INSPIRATION
AND
INCARNATION

INSPIRATION
AND
INCARNATION

Evangelicals and the Problem
of the Old Testament

Peter Enns

Baker Academic
Grand Rapids, Michigan

©2005 by Peter Enns

Published by Baker Academic
a division of Baker Publishing Group
P.O. Box 6287, Grand Rapids, MI 49516-6287
www.bakeracademic.com

Second printing, February 2006

Printed in the United States of America

Library of Congress Cataloging-in-Publication Data
Enns, Peter, 1961–
    Inspiration and incarnation : evangelicals and the problem of the Old Testament / Peter Enns.
        p.   cm.
    Includes bibliographical references and indexes.
    ISBN 10: 0-8010-2730-6
    ISBN 978-0-8010-2730-7
    1. Bible. O.T.—Evidences, authority, etc. 2. Bible. O.T.—Criticism, interpretation, etc. 3. Evangelicalism. I. Title.
    BS480.E56 2005
    220.1′3—dc22   2004029186

For
Erich, Elizabeth, and Sophia
"That's a really good question. . . ."

Contents

Preface

The aim of this book is not novelty but synthesis. My focus is twofold: (1) to bring together a variety of data that biblical scholars work with every day for readers who do not have firsthand familiarity with these data and (2) to look at these data with a clear view toward discussing their implications for an evangelical doctrine of Scripture.

Although it is not always made explicit, in working through these issues I lean heavily on the work of many scholars, some of whom are listed in the "Further Reading" sections at the end of each chapter. Also influential has been my own theological tradition, represented by my colleagues at Westminster Theological Seminary, past and present, and the wider tradition of which that institution is a part. This is not to imply that I speak for that institution or tradition. Nevertheless, I am thankful for being part of such a solidly faithful group that does not shy away from some difficult yet basic questions and with whom I am able to have frank and open discussions. This does not happen at every institution, and I do not take that privilege for granted.

Biblical citations are quoted from the New International Version, except where noted. Apocryphal material (i.e., the Wisdom of Solomon in chapter 4) is quoted from the New Revised Standard Version. With the exception of the *Code of Hammurabi*, which is quoted from James Pritchard's *Ancient Near Eastern Texts* (though I have modernized it in places), the ancient Near Eastern texts in chapter 2 are quoted from *The Context of Scripture* by W. W. Hallo and K. L. Younger. In chapter 4, the pseudepigraphal texts are quoted from James Charlesworth's *Old Testament Pseudepigrapha* and the Dead Sea Scrolls from G. Vermes's *Dead Sea Scrolls in English*. Full bibliographic data for these works is given in the "Further Reading" sections at the end of the respective chapters.

Key terms and concepts, especially those that may be unfamiliar to the reader, are defined in the glossary and appear in boldface type on first mention in the text.

I would like to take this opportunity to thank my editor, Jim Kinney, who has spent much time interacting with me on this project. My former student, Shannon Geiger, now a church planter in Dallas, Texas, spent many hours reading an earlier draft of this book and made numerous invaluable suggestions. This is a better book for her efforts.

I believe with all my heart that honesty with oneself is a central component to spiritual growth. God honors our honest questions. He is not surprised by them, nor is he ashamed to be our God when we pose them. He is our God, not because of the questions we ask (or refrain from asking), but because he has united us to the risen Christ. And being a part of God's family is ultimately a gift to us, not something to be obtained by us. God has freed us in Christ and made us his children. And, as all children do, we ask a lot of questions.

Abbreviations

RSV   Holy Bible: Revised Standard Version
TNIV   Holy Bible: Today's New International Version
Wis.   Wisdom of Solomon

1

Getting Our Bearings

What I Hope to Accomplish in This Book

The purpose of this book is to bring an evangelical doctrine of Scripture into conversation with the implications generated by some important themes in modern biblical scholarship—particularly Old Testament scholarship—over the past 150 years. To put it this way is to suggest that such a conversation has not taken place, at least not to the degree that it could have. It is not to suggest, however, that evangelical biblical scholarship has not engaged many of these issues responsibly on an academic level. There is no question that evangelical scholars have made many excellent contributions, for example, in archeological, historical, and textual studies.

In my view, however, what is needed is not simply for evangelicals to work *in* these areas, but to engage the *doctrinal implications* that work in these areas raises. Without wanting to overstate the matter, I know or hear of a fair number of Christians who conclude that the contemporary state of biblical scholarship makes an evangelical faith unviable. These are the primary readers I envision for this book, those who desire to maintain a vibrant and reverent doctrine of Scripture, but who find it difficult to do so because they find familiar and conventional approaches to newer problems to be unhelpful.

On the one hand, I am very eager to affirm that many evangelical instincts are correct and should be maintained, for example, the con-

viction that the Bible is ultimately from God and that it is God's gift to
the church. Any theories concerning Scripture that do not arise from
these fundamental instincts are unacceptable. On the other hand, how
the evangelical church *fleshes out* its doctrine of Scripture will always
have somewhat of a provisional quality to it. This is not to say that
each generation must disregard the past and start afresh, formulating
ever-new doctrines, bowing to all the latest fads. But it is to say that at
such time when new evidence comes to light, or old evidence is seen in
a new light, we must be willing to engage that evidence and adjust our
doctrine accordingly.

Such adjustments do not simply represent recent developments. One
need only think of Copernicus (1473–1543), the Polish astronomer who
determined that the earth revolved around the sun, a heretical view at
the time. The Catholic Church resisted this evidence for many years
(Galileo was imprisoned for it in 1633). Eventually, however, the previ-
ously held "biblical" geocentric view was abandoned by the church.
This is just one of many examples that could be given where evidence
outside the Bible, in this case scientific, affected how we view the Bible.
Or to put it better, the scientific evidence showed us that the worldview
of the biblical authors affected what they thought and wrote, and so the
worldviews of the biblical authors must be taken into consideration in
matters of biblical interpretation.

Reassessment of doctrine on the basis of external evidence, therefore,
is nothing new. To state it differently, our topic is the age-old question
of the relationship between **special revelation** (the Bible) and **general
revelation** (creation, i.e., everything else). My concern is that, at least on
a popular level, a defensive approach to the evidence tends to dominate
the evangelical conversation. For recent generations of evangelicals, this
tendency has its roots in certain developments that occurred in biblical scholarship during the nineteenth century and made headlines in
the so-called modernist/fundamentalist controversies around the turn
of the twentieth century (e.g., the Scopes monkey trial). The effects of
these developments can still be felt today. Much of the evangelical theological landscape of the twentieth and into the twenty-first centuries
was dominated by a "battle for the Bible." The terms are familiar: liberal
vs. conservative, modernist vs. fundamentalist, mainline vs. evangelical,
progressive vs. traditionalist. Such labels may serve some purpose, but
they more often serve to entrench rather than enlighten.

I want to make it clear here at the outset that this book is not intended
to solve "Bible difficulties" here and there, nor is it to perpetuate the
debate by defending either side of the debate, nor to find a middle way
between them. My aim is somewhat more foundational while at the
same time being far less ambitious. I want to contribute to a growing

opinion that what is needed is to move beyond both sides by thinking of better ways to account for some of the data, while at the same time having a vibrant, positive view of Scripture as God's word. By focusing on three problems raised by the modern study of the Old Testament, my hope is to suggest ways in which our conversation can be shifted somewhat, so that what are often *perceived* as problems with the Old Testament are put into a different perspective. To put it another way, my aim is to allow the collective evidence to affect not just how we understand a biblical passage or story here and there within the parameters of earlier doctrinal formulations. Rather, I want to move beyond that by allowing the evidence to affect how we think about what Scripture as a whole *is*.

The end result, I truly hope, will be to provide a theological paradigm for people who know instinctively that the Bible is God's word, but for whom reading the Bible has already become a serious theological problem—perhaps even a crisis. I have come across many Christians for whom this clash between the biblical world and the modern world is a very real issue. The Bible is central to their lives, but sometimes evangelical defenses of the Bible are exercises in special pleading, attempts to hold on to comfortable ideas despite evidence that makes such ideas problematic. It is precisely the ineffectiveness of certain ways of thinking about the Bible that can sometimes cause significant cognitive dissonance for Christians who love and want to hold on to their Bibles, but who also feel the weight of certain kinds of evidence.

With this in mind, one of the central themes of this book is this:

The problems many of us feel regarding the Bible may have less to do with the Bible itself and more to do with our own preconceptions.

I have found again and again that listening to how the Bible itself behaves and suspending preconceived notions (as much as that is possible) about how we think the Bible ought to behave is refreshing, creative, exciting, and spiritually rewarding.

To work through this process, I want to focus on three issues that have not been handled well in evangelical theology. These three issues are not based on fanciful, trendy theories, but on evidence that comes from within the Bible itself, as well as from the world surrounding the Bible:

1. *The Old Testament and other literature from the ancient world*: Why does the Bible in places look a lot like the literature of Israel's ancient neighbors? Is the Old Testament really that unique? Does it not just reflect the ancient world in which it was produced?

If the Bible is the word of God, why does it fit so nicely in the ancient world?

2. *Theological diversity in the Old Testament*: Why do different parts of the Old Testament say different things about the same thing? It really seems as if there are contradictions, or at least large differences of opinion, in the Old Testament.

3. *The way in which the New Testament authors handle the Old Testament*: Why do the New Testament authors handle the Old Testament in such odd ways? It looks like they just take the Old Testament passages out of context.

Each of these three points has its own chapter in this book. To those perhaps more familiar with biblical studies, the importance of these three issues will be immediately recognizable. The latter two problems are generated directly by the Bible itself. And for at least the first and last items, older approaches to the Bible do not always take the extrabiblical evidence into account. This is partly the case because these extrabiblical evidences have made their presence felt only over the past 150 years or so; older approaches to understanding the Bible were already well established before this evidence came to light.

Why these three issues? I could have brought others into the discussion or arranged the evidence in different ways, but I choose these three for what I think is a very good reason. Each of these issues, in its own way, presents challenges to traditional, evangelical views about Scripture.

The first issue deals with the Bible's *uniqueness*. It is a common expectation, often implicit, that for the Bible to be God's word, it should be unique, that is, it should not bear striking similarities to the literature of other ancient peoples.

The second concerns the Bible's *integrity*, its trustworthiness. It is a common expectation that the Bible be unified in its outlook, be free of diverse views, if we are being asked to trust it as God's word (does not God have just one opinion on things?).

The third deals with the Bible's *interpretation*. To modern readers, the New Testament authors sometimes seem to interpret the Old Testament in fanciful ways, seemingly unconcerned about the meaning of the Old Testament in its original context. This seems to make the whole issue of Old Testament interpretation highly subjective. Should this have an effect on how Christians today handle the Old Testament?

Regardless of how we organize the data, the issue before us is not how we handle this verse or this issue, one at a time. Rather, what needs to happen is that we take a step back from the details and allow these issues to challenge us on a more fundamental level. What is needed is a way of thinking about Scripture where these kinds of issues are addressed from a very different perspective—where these kinds of problems cease being problems and become windows that open up new ways of understanding. It is not enough simply to say that the Bible is the word of God or that it is inspired or to apply some other label. The issue is how these descriptions of the Bible bear fruit when we touch down in one part of the Bible or another. How does the study of Scripture in the contemporary world affect how we flesh out descriptions such as "word of God" or "inspired"?

A Way toward Addressing the Problem: The Incarnational Analogy

I do not want to suggest that difficult problems have simple solutions. What I want to offer, instead, is a proper starting point for discussing these problems, one that, if allowed to run its course, will reorient us to see these problems in a better light. This starting point can be traced back to the early centuries of the church and can be applied to modern issues with considerable profit. The starting point for our discussion is the following: *as Christ is both God and human, so is the Bible*. In other words, we are to think of the Bible in the same way that Christians think about Jesus. Christians confess that Jesus is both God and human at the same time. He is not half-God and half-human. He is not sometimes one and other times the other. He is not essentially one and only apparently the other. Rather, one of the central doctrines of the Christian faith, worked out as far back as the Council of Chalcedon in AD 451, is that Jesus is 100 percent God and 100 percent human—at the same time.

This way of thinking of Christ is analogous to thinking about the Bible. In the same way that Jesus is—*must be*—both God and human, the Bible is also a divine and human book. Although Jesus was "*God* with us," he still completely assumed the cultural trappings of the world in which he lived. In fact, this is what is implied in "God *with us*." Perhaps this is part of what the author of Hebrews had in mind when he said that Christ was "made like his brothers in every way" (Heb. 2:17). Jesus was a first-century Jew. The languages of the time (**Hebrew**, **Greek**, **Aramaic**) were his languages. Their customs were his customs. He fit, he belonged, he was one of them.

So, too, the Bible. It belonged in the ancient worlds that produced it. It was not an abstract, otherworldly book, dropped out of heaven. It was *connected to* and therefore *spoke to* those ancient cultures. The encultured qualities of the Bible, therefore, are not extra elements that we can discard to get to the real point, the timeless truths. Rather, precisely because Christianity is a historical religion, God's word reflects the various historical moments in which Scripture was written. God acted and spoke in history. As we learn more and more about that history, we must gladly address the implications of that history for how we view the Bible, that is, what we should expect from it.

This way of thinking about the Bible is referred to differently by different theologians. The term I prefer is *incarnational analogy*: Christ's incarnation is analogous to Scripture's "incarnation." As with any analogy, one could highlight places where the analogy does not quite fit. Moreover, we must reckon with the incarnation of Christ itself being mysterious; one could rightly question the merit of using an ultimately unexplainable entity to explain something else! That being said, my starting point is the orthodox Christian confession, however mysterious it is, that Jesus of Nazareth is the God-man. The long-standing identification between Christ the word and Scripture the word is central to how I think through the issues raised in this book: *How does Scripture's full humanity and full divinity affect what we should expect from Scripture?*

The ancient heresy of Docetism stated that Christ was fully divine and only *seemed* to be human (the Greek verb *dokein* ["to seem"] is the root of the word *Docetism*). The Council of Chalcedon rightly concluded that if Christ only appeared to be human, then the death and resurrection are not real. And, if that is the case, then there is no forgiveness of sins. Although I am in no way implying that people who do not see things as I do are heretics, there is an analogy to be drawn here. What some ancient Christians were saying about Christ, the Docetic heresy, is similar to the mistake that other Christians have made (and continue to make) about Scripture: it comes from God, and the marks of its humanity are only apparent, to be explained away. Of course, no evangelical would willingly or consciously put it that way, but, when confronted with some of the problems addressed in this book, "scriptural docetism" rears its head. But the human marks of the Bible are *everywhere*, *thoroughly integrated* into the nature of Scripture itself. Ignoring these marks or explaining them away takes at least as much energy as listening to them and learning from them.

The human dimension of Scripture is, therefore, part of what makes Scripture Scripture. But it is precisely this dimension that can create problems for modern Christian readers, because it can make the Bible seem less unique, less "Bible-like," than we might have supposed.

Here are some of these human marks of Scripture (focusing mainly on the Old Testament). Most of these will not be discussed in the following chapters. I mention them at this juncture only in an effort to orient us to the general discussion:

1. *The Bible was written in Hebrew and Greek (with a little Aramaic).* This is stating the obvious and hardly poses a theological problem. Still, there is a lesson to be learned. Neither Hebrew, Aramaic, nor Greek has any special quality about it that makes it somehow specially suited to be the conveyor of God's word. This may have been thought to be the case at one time, but it is a position that cannot be held in light of modern developments in linguistics. We know, for example, that Hebrew is simply one ancient **Semitic language** that has a lot in common with many other ancient languages, such as Aramaic, **Moabite**, **Edomite**, **Ammonite**, **Ugaritic**, and **Phoenician**. All of these ancient languages existed during Old Testament times, and some of them are in fact quite a bit older.

   The point is made more clearly in the case of Greek. Until the late nineteenth century some considered the Greek of the New Testament to be a unique, heavenly language. This was thought to be the case because the style of the New Testament was very different from that found in Greek philosophical texts or in Homer's *Iliad* and *Odyssey*. So some concluded that the Greek of the New Testament was a special "Holy Spirit language" prepared by God to convey his word. This was a maintainable position (although still conjectural) until archeologists began unearthing documents written in a Greek style similar to the New Testament. And these documents were not concerned with anything official, nor were they meant for public consumption. Rather they were written by everyday, insignificant people about things that were never intended to be handed down through the ages, such as letters and contracts. Even in the language of the Bible, God demonstrates that he is "one of us."

   For the Old Testament or New Testament, the point is the same. That the Bible is written in human language, and in the common tongue at that, is already an example of God "incarnating" himself. He adopts the current cultural conventions and uses them for his purpose. The languages are not specially designed to carry God's word, but God makes those languages adequate to do so.

2. *The Old Testament world was a world of temples, priests, and sacrifice.* Israel was not the first nation, nor the last, to have a religious system centered on temples, priests, and sacrifices. Such things were woven into the fabric of the ancient societies of the Mesopotamian world.

3. *Israel as well as the surrounding nations had prophets that mediated divine will to them.* The role of the prophets in the Old Testament is a very important one. They were God's mouthpieces to Israel

and the kings. But prophecy was by no means unique to ancient Israel. Every ancient society had prophets and seers.

4. *Through much of its history, Israel was ruled by kings, as were the nations around it.* In fact, when it comes to kingship, Israel was a "Jacob-come-lately." A refrain in 1 Samuel is that the Israelites wanted a king like "all the other nations" (8:5). Was Israel simply mimicking the political structures of the surrounding peoples?

5. *Israel's legal system has some striking similarities with those of surrounding nations.* When compared side by side with other ancient legal codes, such as the Babylonian *Code of Hammurabi* (see chapter 2), one can see significant similarities between the Mosaic law and those of other—older—nations.

All of these examples (and a good many more) have been brought to light by linguistic, historical, and archeological investigations that began to flourish around the middle of the nineteenth century. In other words, these are problems that are specific to people who live in the modern world, where scholarly investigation demonstrates time and time again that the Bible is firmly situated in the ancient world in which it was produced.

What is so helpful about the incarnational analogy is that it reorients us to see that the Bible's "situatedness" is not a lamentable or embarrassing situation, but a positive one:

> *That the Bible, at every turn, shows how "connected" it is to its own world is a necessary consequence of God incarnating himself.*

When God reveals himself, he always does so to people, which means that he must speak and act in ways that they will understand. People are time bound, and so God adopts that characteristic if he wishes to reveal himself. We can put this even a bit more strongly:

> *It is essential to the very nature of revelation that the Bible is not unique to its environment. The human dimension of Scripture is essential to its being Scripture.*

This, I argue, is the proper starting point for looking at the relationship between the Bible and the issues we will discuss in this book.

That the Bible is so easily situated in its ancient context is a source of difficulty for many modern readers. A conclusion some draw is that the Bible is, therefore, *merely* just like any other ancient book. On the other hand, the conservative reaction tends toward minimizing some of the more challenging of these human marks of Scripture, thus accenting its uniqueness *over against* the ancient world. What I propose, however, is an approach that accepts neither alternative as offering the final word. That the Bible bears an unmistakable human stamp does *not* lead to the necessary conclusion that it is *merely* the words of humans rather than the word of God. To those who hold such a position the question might be asked, "How *else* would you have expected God to speak? In ways wholly *disconnected* to the ancient world? Who would have understood him?"

And to those who fear the human stamp as somehow dirtying the Bible, marring its perfect divine quality, I say, "If you wouldn't say that about Jesus (and you shouldn't), don't think that way about the Bible. Both Christ and his word are human through and through." In fact, it is precisely by having the Son become human that God demonstrates his great love. Is it so much of a stretch, then, to say that the human nature of Scripture is likewise a gift rather than a problem? Of course, simply saying this does not make the issues float away, but it is the proper way to begin addressing those issues.

It is somewhat ironic, it seems to me, that both liberals and conservatives make the same error. They both assume that something worthy of the title *word of God* would look different from what we actually have. The one accents the human marks and makes them absolute. The other wishes the human marks were not as pronounced as they were. They share a similar opinion that nothing worthy of being called God's word would look so common, so human, so recognizable. But, when God speaks, he speaks in ways we would understand. With this in mind, we can now look at some of the evidence that has been part of the scholarly conversation for several generations, not to determine *whether* the Bible is God's word, but to see more clearly *how* it is God's word.

Further Reading

Orr, James. *Revelation and Inspiration*. London: Duckworth, 1910. Reprinted Grand Rapids: Eerdmans, 1952.

> A relatively early attempt to understand the nature of Scripture from a conservative perspective but one that also engages constructively the intellectual climate of the time.

Rogerson, John. *Old Testament Criticism in the Nineteenth Century: England and Germany*. Philadelphia: Fortress, 1985.

> A helpful, fact-filled book on the major European critical Old Testament scholars of the nineteenth century.

Smyth, J. Patterson. *How God Inspired the Bible: Thoughts for the Present Disquiet*. New York: James Pott, 1892.

> Written during the so-called modernist/fundamentalist controversy and addressing many of the same issues addressed here. What is perhaps most striking about Smyth's book, besides the honesty and spiritual sensitivity of the author (he was both a professor and pastor), is the reminder that an incarnational approach to Scripture was employed generations ago to address the problems introduced by the modern study of the Bible.

Warfield, B. B. "The Divine and Human in the Bible." Pages 51–58 in Warfield's *Evolution, Science, and Scripture: Selected Writings*. Edited by Mark A. Noll and David N. Livingston. Grand Rapids: Baker, 2000.

> Originally written in 1894, this brief article is a wonderfully succinct explication of Warfield's notion of "concursus" in the Bible, which is the working together of human and divine elements to produce the Bible. Warfield taught at Princeton Theological Seminary until his death in 1921 and leaves a legacy of informed, scholarly defense of traditional Christian positions.

2

The Old Testament and Ancient Near Eastern Literature

The Impact of Akkadian Literature

An Important Discovery

Between the years 1848 and 1876, archeologists working in the library of King Ashurbanipal (668–627 BC) in ancient Nineveh (the capital city of ancient **Assyria**, located in modern-day Iraq) discovered thousands of clay tablets with markings on them. These markings had only fairly recently come to light, and so their significance was not immediately known. Soon these tablets were to have a profound impact on biblical studies. They told stories that had not been read for over two thousand years. Some of these tablets contained an ancient account of the creation of the world and the flood written by a people similar to the ancient Israelites but still very distinct from them. British archeologist George Smith eventually published a translation of these tablets. It is not an overstatement to say that how people viewed the Bible would never be the same again.

The language these tablets were written in came to be known as **Akkadian**, which is the English translation of the term the speakers of this language used themselves, *Akkadum*. Akkadian was the main language of many ancient Near Eastern (frequently abbreviated **ANE** in the scholarly

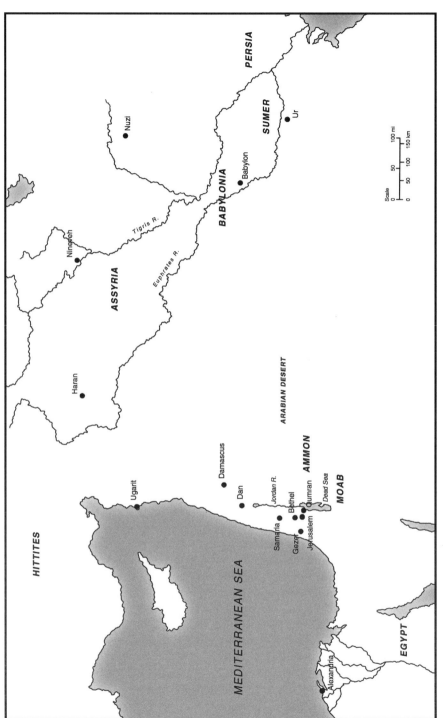

The Ancient Near East

literature) cultures spanning the third, second, and first millennia BC. Most importantly for us, it was the language of two prominent nations known to us from the Old Testament: Assyria and **Babylon**.

Among these Akkadian tablets were found such things as legal texts, economic texts, historical texts, and letters. From these texts we gain many valuable insights into what life was like in the ancient Near East three thousand to four thousand years ago. But what was most interesting—and a bit unsettling—were the *religious texts* found there. In many places, these texts sound very much like things we read in the Old Testament (a phenomenon often referred to as ancient Near Eastern parallels to the Old Testament). For Christians, particularly for a traditional Christian understanding of Scripture, this is where the trouble started, particularly with respect to the creation and flood stories found there. The doctrinal implications of these discoveries have not yet been fully worked out in evangelical theology.

The Akkadian texts we will look at below have been chosen because they are relatively well known. They are also particularly suited to illustrate the impact that these discoveries have had on our understanding of the Old Testament. After looking at these Akkadian texts, we will look at several texts from other ancient cultures and one nonbiblical Hebrew text from Israel itself. At this point, I will present these ancient texts with very little commentary. After looking at these examples, we will summarize the issues that these texts raise for us. Next we will see how these issues have been handled in the past, and then suggest how the incarnational analogy can offer a better way of handling them today.

Creation: **Enuma Elish**

Enuma Elish has been referred to as the "Babylonian Genesis." The title of the story is a modern convention derived from the opening words of the story, *Enuma Elish* ("when on high"). The version found in Ashurbanipal's library consists of seven tablets and dates to the seventh century BC, but it is recognized by scholars that the story itself is much older. Determining the precise age of the story is based on a combination of linguistic and historical factors, but a date sometime in the second millennium BC is the consensus position. Specifically, the earliest likely date is the eighteenth century BC, for it is around this time that the god Marduk (mentioned prominently in *Enuma Elish*) seemed to be raised to a prominent status. Some scholars suggest a slightly later date (i.e., fourteenth to twelfth centuries).

In any case, the extant copy of *Enuma Elish*, therefore, does not in any way indicate when the story *originated*. Moreover, there was certainly a period of oral transmission prior to written records in the ancient world. This is all the more certain in view of general literacy not being a widespread phenomenon in the second millennium BC. What concerns us here, however, is not setting a firm date for *Enuma Elish*, but understanding the similarities between it and Genesis and what they imply.

The degree to which Genesis and *Enuma Elish* are truly parallel is a debated point, but some of the more agreed upon similarities are the following:

1. The sequence of the days of creation is similar, including the creation of the firmament, dry land, luminaries, and humanity, followed by rest.
2. Darkness precedes the creative acts.
3. There is a division of the waters (waters above and below the firmament).
4. Light exists before the creation of the sun, moon, and stars.

I should be quick to point out, however, that Genesis did not simply copy from *Enuma Elish*, as if the Hebrew author of Genesis had a copy of this Akkadian text in front of him and borrowed from it. Furthermore, at each of the points mentioned above, the Babylonian and biblical creation stories are both similar and dissimilar. Hence, the consensus scholarly position is to not draw a direct line of dependence from Genesis to *Enuma Elish*, and I concur wholeheartedly. When these tablets were discovered, there was a tendency to exaggerate their influence—in the early nineteenth century this was known as the "Bible and Babel" controversy. As time went on, scholars generally began to develop a more sober appreciation for the relevance of the Babylonian material, mainly the recognition of these dissimilarities.

One of the chief differences is that the Babylonian story depicts the creation of the world as a cosmic battle between the god Marduk and his great-great-grandmother, the goddess Tiamat. Tiamat and her husband, Apsu, were the parents of all the gods. Apsu intended to kill his divine offspring, but his grandson Ea intervened and, in an act of trickery, killed Apsu. In time Tiamat grew angry and planned to go to war against the other gods. Ea's son Marduk then fought Tiamat and killed her. From her slain body Marduk created heaven and earth, an act that won him notoriety and thus eventually the head seat at the Babylonian pantheon. (The purpose of *Enuma Elish* seems to be to justify the worship of Marduk as the supreme god.)

Despite these differences, however, the problem remains. However different the two stories may be, they unquestionably share a common way of speaking about the beginning of the world; both Genesis and *Enuma Elish* "breathe the same air." Whether or not the author of Genesis was familiar with the text known to us as *Enuma Elish*, he was certainly working within a similar conceptual world. So, as unwise as it is to equate the two, it is also ill advised to make such a sharp distinction between them that the clear similarities are brushed aside. The Genesis account must be understood in its ancient context, and stories like *Enuma Elish* help us glimpse what that context looked like.

One could suggest that the purpose of Genesis was to contrast such ancient Near Eastern stories as *Enuma Elish*. The God of Genesis simply *speaks* things into being. It is reasonable to suggest that the Genesis story is meant to be contrasted to the reigning Babylonian ideology; that is, one could argue that an important purpose of the Genesis story is to argue that the God of Israel is *truly* mighty and that he is *solely* and *fully* in control of the cosmos. His creation of the world is an act of his will, not the result of a power struggle within a dysfunctional divine family. We must remember that such a contrast can be fully appreciated only when we first acknowledge that the Genesis story is firmly rooted in the worldview of its time. We will return to the implications of this later in the chapter after we look at the rest of our examples.

Flood: **Atrahasis** *and* **Gilgamesh**

Whatever similarities there are between Genesis and *Enuma Elish*, the ancient Near Eastern parallels concerning the flood story are more striking. The *Atrahasis* and *Gilgamesh* epics both relate stories of a cataclysmic flood. They are not the only ancient versions of the story; there are other Akkadian versions as well as an even older **Sumerian** version. *Atrahasis* and *Gilgamesh* are the most relevant to Genesis, however.

The earliest copies of *Atrahasis* date to the seventeenth century BC. It must also be remembered, as in the case of *Enuma Elish*, that the date of the text that archeologists found tells us little about how old the story itself might be. *Atrahasis*, which is also the name of the story's Noah-like figure, tells of a flood that was the result of the decree of the god Enlil to destroy humans because they were making too much noise. Atrahasis, through the help of the god Ea, escapes the wrath of Enlil by building a large boat in which to save humanity.

The earliest copies of *Gilgamesh* are Sumerian and are dated to the first half of the second millennium BC. Some argue for a date in the middle of the third millennium. Like *Enuma Elish*, the form in which we know it now stems from the early part of the first millennium BC and survives in twelve tablets. The title of this story is also the name of the main character. After the death of his dear friend Enkidu, Gilgamesh takes a journey to find the secret of immortality. This quest leads him to the hero of this version of the flood story, known as Utnapishtim, of whom he makes a request for help. Alas, Gilgamesh does not find the immortality he seeks, but amid his conversations with Utnapishtim, the flood story is recounted to him in some detail.

Here are some of the key lines in these two flood stories that parallel Genesis. I quote them in some detail so as to give a sense of the impact of these texts. Brackets and dots in the translations below refer to those portions of the stone tablets that either have become worn over the millennia or have broken off. Where scholars can make good guesses, the brackets are filled in. If not, they are left empty. Words in parentheses are not in the original but clearly implied. Spaces between lines indicate portions of the story left out because they are not relevant for our purposes here.

Atrahasis

Flee the house, build a boat,
Forsake possessions, and save life.
The boat which you build,
[   ] be equal [   ]

Pure (animals) he sl[aughtered, cattle]. . . .
Fat (animals) [he killed, sheep(?)]. . . .
He chose [and brought on] board.
The [birds] flying in the heavens,
The cattle(?) [and   the cat]tle god.

[   ] His family he brought on board.

He brought pitch to seal his door.

Gilgamesh

The ship which you shall build,
Let her dimensions be measured off.
Let her width and length be equal.

Ten dozen cubits each was the height of her walls,
Ten dozen cubits each were the edges around her.

Thrice 3600 measures of pitch I poured in the oven,
Thrice 3600 measures of tar did [I pour out] inside her.

What living creatures I had I loaded upon her.
I made go aboard all my family and kin,
Beasts of the steppe, wild animals of the steppe.

The sea grew calm, the tempest grew still, the deluge ceased.
I looked at the weather, stillness reigned,
And all of mankind had turned into clay.
The landscape was flat as a terrace.
I opened the hatch, daylight fell upon my face.

The boat rested on Mount Nimush,
Mount Nimush held the boat fast, not allowing it to move.
One day, a second day Mount Nimush held the boat fast, not
    allowing it to move.
A third day, a fourth day Mount Nimush held the boat fast, not
    allowing it to move.
A fifth day, a sixth day Mount Nimush held the boat fast, not
    allowing it to move.
When the seventh day arrives,
I released a dove to go free,
The dove went and returned,
No landing place came to view, it turned back.
I released a swallow to go free,
The swallow went and returned,
No landing place came to view, it turned back.
I sent a raven to go free,
The raven went forth, saw the ebbing of the waters,
It ate, circled, left droppings, did not turn back.

Reading these stories side by side with Genesis 6–8 makes clear the extent of the similarities between *Atrahasis/Gilgamesh* and Genesis. As with
Enuma Elish, one should not conclude that the biblical account is directly
dependent on these flood stories. Still, the obvious similarities between them
indicates a connection on some level. Perhaps one borrowed from the other,
or perhaps all of these stories have older precursors. The second option is
quite possible, since, as mentioned above, there exists a Sumerian flood
story that is considered older than either the Akkadian or biblical versions.
In either case, the question remains how the Akkadian evidence influences
our understanding of the historical nature of the biblical story.

Israel's Ancestors: Nuzi

Nuzi is the name of an ancient city that flourished during the middle
of the second millennium BC in what is modern-day northern Iraq. The
tablets found there (beginning in the mid-1920s) are not stories but

legal, administrative, and economic texts and date to the fourteenth and fifteenth centuries BC. This may not sound exciting, but what they give us is a feel for the world in which Israel's first ancestors (Abraham and Sarah, Isaac and Rebekah, Jacob and Rachel, and Jacob's twelve sons) lived, along with some other episodes.

Before we look at some of these examples, I must introduce a word of caution. In the early decades of research into the Nuzi material, far too much was made of the evidence with respect to establishing the historicity of Abraham. What were once thought to be clear parallels between Nuzi and Genesis have been discredited or at least nuanced with other ancient Near Eastern material. I do not want to give the false impression that my comments here are reverting back to an earlier view. My point in bringing up the Nuzi material is that it helps make some of the customs in Genesis *understandable*; that is, the Nuzi texts, as well as texts from other peoples and periods of the ancient Near East, help establish the ancient Near Eastern "feel" of Genesis.

There is no standard English collected edition of the Nuzi tablets, so I merely list some of the more generally agreed upon parallels between the Nuzi culture and the stories of Israel's first ancestors in Genesis:

1. In the story of Abraham, we read that he and his wife Sarah were childless. Abraham adopts Eliezer of Damascus to be his heir (Gen. 15:2–3). Later, in Genesis 16:1–4, Sarah gives her handmaiden Hagar to Abraham in order to bear him an heir (Ishmael). When Isaac is later born to Sarah, that younger child becomes the heir in place of Ishmael, even though he is the younger child. The Nuzi tablets, as well as texts from later periods, record similar legal situations.
2. When Isaac married Rebekah, Rebekah's brother, Laban, handled the negotiations but asked her if she consented (Gen. 28–31). But when Laban arranged the marriage of his daughters to Jacob (29:15–30), his daughters were not consulted. The same situation is represented in Nuzi contracts: when a brother draws up the marriage contract, the woman is consulted, but not if the father draws up the contract.
3. The story of Judah and Tamar in Genesis 38 illustrates the practice of levirate marriage found also in the Nuzi tablets. A widow cannot remarry outside her deceased husband's family. It is the responsibility of the dead husband's brother to carry on his brother's line by marrying the widow.
4. In the Joseph story, Joseph's older brothers are jealous of him because they think that their father, Jacob, will choose him as his heir rather than the oldest brother (Gen. 37). The Nuzi tablets indicate that it was within a father's right to choose a younger son as the heir. This suggests that Joseph's brothers' fears were legitimate.

5. In Genesis 31:50, Laban charges Jacob, with God as his witness, not to take any other wives besides his daughters. A similar prohibition is found in numerous Nuzi marriage contracts.

Again, the Nuzi documents are helpful in providing a general historical context in which the stories of Israel's earliest ancestors would have taken place. But there is another side to the issue. If these biblical stories are so at home in ancient **Mesopotamia**, the reasonable question is raised of how *different* the Bible really is. If the Bible reflects these ancient customs and practices, in what sense can we speak of it as revelation?

Law: The Code of Hammurabi

Hammurabi was a Babylonian king who ruled in the eighteenth century BC. During his reign he enacted a code of law, which was discovered in 1901–2 by French archeologists.

The *Code of Hammurabi* is fairly long, containing just under three hundred laws. There are many similarities between these laws and some of the Old Testament laws. Many of the similarities concern the topics discussed: stealing, property laws, kidnapping, marriage and divorce, loans, holding another's property for safekeeping, personal injury, animals. Some laws have very similar wording to biblical laws. For example, laws 195–214 of the *Code of Hammurabi* deal with personal injuries and find many specific parallels in a portion of Exodus known as the "Book of the Covenant" (Exod. 21–23). A few examples will suffice:

Code of Hammurabi 195–97	Exodus 21:23–25
If a son has struck his father, they shall cut off his hand. If a nobleman has put out the eye of another nobleman, they shall put out his eye. If he has broken another nobleman's bone, they shall break his bone.	But if there is serious injury, you are to take life for life, eye for eye, tooth for tooth, hand for hand, foot for foot, burn for burn, wound for wound, bruise for bruise.

Code of Hammurabi 198–201	Exodus 21:26–27
If he has put out the eye of a commoner or broken the bone of a commoner, he shall pay one silver mina. If he has put out the eye of a nobleman's slave or broken the bone of a nobleman's slave, he shall pay one-half of its value. If a nobleman has knocked out the tooth of his equal, they shall knock out his tooth. If he has knocked out the tooth of a commoner, he shall pay one-third of a silver mina.	If a man hits a manservant or maidservant in the eye and destroys it, he must let the servant go free to compensate for the eye. And if he knocks out the tooth of a manservant or maidservant, he must let the servant go free to compensate for the tooth.

Code of Hammurabi 209	Exodus 21:22
If a nobleman has struck another nobleman's daughter and has caused her to have a miscarriage, he shall pay ten shekels of silver for her fetus.	If men who are fighting hit a pregnant woman and she gives birth prematurely but there is no serious injury, the offender must be fined whatever the woman's husband demands and the court allows.

All three groups concern the law of "an eye for an eye," and all three make distinctions based on the perceived worth of the injured party. Other examples could be noted. The problem these parallels create is obvious to those familiar with the biblical story. According to Exodus, the biblical laws are uttered by God and *revealed* to Moses on Mount Sinai. But (1) the biblical story occurred centuries after Hammurabi, and (2) when compared with the *Code of Hammurabi* (and several other similar law codes of the ancient Near East), the biblical laws look somewhat commonplace. How should this affect how we think about the Old Testament as Scripture?

What we have seen here is only an indication of the importance of these Akkadian texts in shedding light on the Old Testament. So important are these (and other) documents that they have inspired generations of Old Testament scholars to study the Old Testament in its ancient Near Eastern context. Setting the Bible in its historical context has dominated university departments as well as many evangelical schools. This is to be expected: most people interested in the Bible, whether for academic or religious reasons, want to know more about where the Bible came from. Also, for evangelicals, placing the Old Testament in its ancient context sometimes helps to defend the historical nature of the Bible.

The problem, already hinted at above, is that showing how at home the Bible is in the ancient world makes it look less special in some respects—less unique. What can we say about the uniqueness of the Bible when, in so many areas, it bears striking similarities to the beliefs and practices of the other nations? This is precisely where the tension lies: the true faith of Israel and the false faith of her neighbors look similar. Some interpret this evidence as showing that the Bible is merely another example of an ancient religious text—somewhat fanciful and silly by modern standards. The conservative reaction over the last century and a half tends to minimize the ancient Near Eastern setting of the Old Testament, at least where that setting poses challenges to traditional belief. Neither the liberal conclusion ("the Bible is just like any other ancient book") nor the conservative response ("no it's not" or "it only seems that way" or "sometimes yes, sometimes no") addresses the issue adequately, in my opinion.

But before we pursue this line of thinking more fully, it will help to cast our net further to include evidence from cultures of the ancient Near East other than Assyria and Babylon.

Some Other Ancient Near Eastern Texts

Deuteronomy and Hittite Suzerainty Treaties

At various times throughout the twentieth century, archeologists were at work unearthing a culture that was known to us from the Old Testament but that until then had yielded no physical evidence. These were the Hittites, and they lived more or less in what is today Turkey.

Among the finds were treaty documents between kings and their vassals, which are referred to today as suzerain or vassal treaties. (The suzerain is the overlord who claims ruling authority over the vassal, who, in turn, owes obedience to the suzerain.) The structure of these treaties has been compared with the structure of the book of Deuteronomy in general and the Ten Commandments in particular. The biblical texts and the Hittite treaties have many things in common:

1. The treaties begin with a preamble or historical prologue announcing the name of the king and what he has done for the vassals. Thus, the Ten Commandments begin, "I am the LORD your God, who brought you out of Egypt, out of the land of slavery." God announces himself and then reminds the Israelites of what he has done for them.
2. After this introduction the Hittite treaties have some stipulations (or laws) that the vassal is meant to obey, the most important of which is loyalty to the king. This is not unlike the first commandment: "You shall have no other gods before me."
3. The Hittite treaties also included an explicit demand that vassals remain bound by oath to the king, otherwise they will have the gods to answer to. Some understand the third commandment to be functioning in a similar way: "You shall not misuse the name of the LORD your God."
4. Then follows a series of blessings and curses, blessings for those who obey and curses for those who do not. In the Ten Commandments, such a blessing is found in the fifth commandment, to honor one's mother and father: "So that you may live long in the land the LORD your God is giving you."
5. One final parallel concerns the Ten Commandments being written on two tablets. Hittite treaties were written in two copies,

one for the king and the other for the vassal. Although it cannot be proven conclusively, it is very inviting to see the two tablets of the Ten Commandments in the same light. Throughout history, the explanation for why Moses came down from the mountain with two tablets has been that half of the commandments (or perhaps the first four) were on the first tablet and the remaining commandments were on the second. That may be, but the Hittite evidence introduces another possibility: the Israelites were given two *complete* copies of the Ten Commandments. Regardless of how one answers these specific questions, the Hittite evidence affects how one goes about answering them.

Not only the Ten Commandments but the structure of the book of Deuteronomy as a whole also seems to reflect the structure of the Hittite treaties. Each section of Deuteronomy reflects a section of the Hittite treaties:

- preamble (1:1–5)
- historical prologue (1:6–4:49)
- stipulations (laws) (5:1–26:19)
- blessings and curses (27:1–30:20)
- the future (royal successor, among other things) (31:1–34:12)

Not everyone agrees that the Ten Commandments and Deuteronomy directly reflect the Hittite treaties, but quite a few accept some connection between them. Either way, we cannot simply erect a wall between them and say they have nothing to do with one another. The Ten Commandments and Deuteronomy both reflect an accepted manner of documenting how a vassal people are to behave toward their suzerain lord.

David and the Tel Dan Inscription

One of the more interesting and controversial finds in recent years is the Tel Dan Inscription, which was written in Aramaic and is dated to the ninth or eighth century BC. A "tel" (also spelled tell) is an archeological term for a mound of earth under which lie layers upon layers of remains of past cultures (the farther down you go, the further back in time you go). Dan is the name of a well-known biblical city located in the northern part of Israel (Galilee).

The inscription's importance lies in the phrase *house of David*. This may seem insignificant at first blush, but this inscription sparked sharp debate when it first came to light in 1993. If "house of David" refers to King David of Israel (who lived in the tenth century BC), then this inscription is one of the oldest extrabiblical references to a biblical figure. Some debate ensued about precisely what this portion of the inscription means. When the dust finally settled, the opinion that this inscription is a reference to the biblical David became the majority view. Many consider this inscription very significant for supporting the notion that David and his descendants (his "house") were well-known historical figures in their time.

Hezekiah and the Siloam Tunnel Inscription

Around 701 BC, the Assyrian King Sennacherib was about to attack Jerusalem. The residents of Jerusalem were threatened by the commander of Sennacherib's army, who called out to them that, unless they gave themselves up, they would "eat their own filth and drink their own urine" (2 Kings 18:27), that is, their food and water supply would be cut off. In 2 Kings 20:20, which summarizes the life of King Hezekiah of Jerusalem (715–686 BC), we read that Hezekiah had dug a tunnel to bring fresh water into the city:

> As for the other events of Hezekiah's reign, all his achievements and how he made *the pool and the tunnel* by which he brought water into the city, are they not written in the book of the annals of the kings of Judah?

These "annals of the kings of Judah" do not survive to this day. In 1880, however, an inscription was found in a tunnel in Jerusalem. That tunnel led from Gihon Spring (located in the northeast corner of Jerusalem) to the Pool of Siloam (southwest corner). The inscription was found on the wall of the tunnel just a few feet from where the tunnel met the Pool of Siloam. It tells how two groups of diggers began at opposite ends and dug toward each other to meet in the middle. Known as the Siloam Tunnel Inscription, it records the moment when they broke through:

> [The day of] the breach.
> This is the record of how the tunnel was breached.
> While [the excavators were wielding] their pick-axes,
>   each man towards his co-worker,
> and while there were yet three cubits for the brea[ch],
> a voice [was hea]rd
>   each man calling to his co-worker;
> because there was a cavity in the rock (extending)
> from the south to [the north].
> So on the day of the breach,

the excavators struck,
  each man to meet his co-worker,
pick-axe against pick-[a]xe.
Then the water flowed from the spring to the pool,
a distance of one thousand and two hundred cubits.
One hundred cubits was the height of the rock above the heads of the
  excavat[ors].

Although this inscription does not mention Hezekiah or Sennacherib by name, there is little question in anyone's mind that it pertains directly to the digging of the tunnel mentioned in 2 Kings 20:20.

What makes the Siloam Tunnel Inscription somewhat out of the ordinary is that it is not prominently displayed but tucked away several feet inside the tunnel entrance. This strongly suggests that it was not an official royal pronouncement intended to beef up a king's image (as we will see below with the Mesha Inscription). In fact, this ancient inscription may never have been intended to be read by more than just a very few people who would have reason to be in the tunnel. It is, in other words, a piece of history writing "caught off guard." Hence, it is a very important witness to the general historical veracity of the biblical accounts of the reigns of the kings.

Omri and the Mesha Inscription

Mesha was king of ancient Moab (on the east side of the Dead Sea opposite Israel) around 830 BC. He erected a monument recounting his deeds as king. That monument is known to us as the Mesha Inscription or the Moabite Stone. Mesha is mentioned in the Old Testament (2 Kings 3:4–5):

> Now Mesha king of Moab raised sheep, and he had to supply the king of Israel with a hundred thousand lambs and with the wool of a hundred thousand rams. But after Ahab died, the king of Moab rebelled against the king of Israel.

What is so important about the Mesha Inscription is not simply that it provides extrabiblical confirmation of King Mesha of Moab, but that it also mentions King Omri of Israel (Ahab's father):

> Omri was the king of Israel,
> and he oppressed Moab for many days,
> for Kemosh was angry with his land.
> And his son succeeded him,
> and he said—he too—

"I will oppress Moab!"
In my days did he say [so],
but I looked down on him and on his house,
and Israel has gone to ruin, yes, it has gone to ruin for ever!
And Omri had taken possession of the whole la[n]d of Medeba,
and he lived there (in) his days and half the days of his son, forty years,
but Kemosh [resto]red it in my days.
And I built Baal Meon,
and I made in it a water reservoir,
and I built Kiriathaim. (lines 5–9)

Clearly Omri had been giving Mesha considerable trouble, but Mesha finally asserted himself and fought back (as indicated in the biblical account). As a whole, the Mesha Inscription seems to be an attempt to vindicate Mesha's reputation. Regardless, along with the Tel Dan Inscription and the Siloam Tunnel Inscription, the Mesha Inscription is an important extrabiblical parallel that gives us a fuller understanding of things recorded in the Bible.

Proverbs and the Instruction of Amenemope

The last ancient Near Eastern parallel we will look at concerns the book of Proverbs. One portion of Proverbs is very similar to a body of Egyptian wisdom literature known as the *Instruction of Amenemope*. Beginning in Proverbs 22:17 we see a change from what has gone before. Specifically, 22:17–24:22 contains more or less commands, whereas what comes before are wise "observations on life." For example, compare 22:16 (observation) to 22:17 (command):

> He who oppresses the poor to increase his wealth
>   and he who gives gifts to the rich—both come to poverty. (22:16)

> Pay attention and listen to the sayings of the wise;
>   apply your heart to what I teach. (22:17)

In fact, 22:17 begins with a title, "Sayings of the Wise," which seems to separate it from what comes before. (Actually, in the Hebrew Old Testament, the words *sayings of the wise* are tucked into the middle of 22:17, which is clearly a scribal mistake. The Greek translation of the Old Testament, the **Septuagint**, has it right by keeping the words at the beginning of the verse. English translations correctly follow the Septuagint here.)

This section, Proverbs 22:17–24:22, bears striking similarities to the *Instruction of Amenemope*. One of the more noticeable parallels concerns

22:20: "Have I not written thirty sayings for you." There is some discussion about whether the Hebrew word does in fact mean thirty, but it is widely accepted that this is certainly the case (the New International Version, for example, adopts this translation). Likewise the *Instruction of Amenemope* is organized into thirty "chapters" (or sections).

More specifically, there are a number of specific similarities between the biblical and Egyptian wisdom texts. The parallels below are between *Amenemope* 3.9–16 and Proverbs 22:17–18:

Instruction of Amenemope	Book of Proverbs
your ears	your ear
hear	listen
the sayings	the sayings
your heart	your heart
it is beneficial	it is pleasing
in the casket of your belly	in your belly
for your tongue	on your lips

There are other parallels between the two, but this should be enough to make the point. The conclusion that has gained the widest agreement is this: (1) Proverbs 22:17–24:22 and *Amenemope* are clearly connected in some way. In other words, they do not look similar by accident. (2) *Amenemope* is older (about 1200 BC), which suggests that the author of Proverbs likely knew of and was in some direct sense dependent upon this Egyptian text.

What Exactly Is the Problem?

So, what is the point of looking at these ancient texts? I chose these texts because they represent different kinds of problems for Christians today who think about their Bible. The impact of these texts leads to questions like these:

1. Does the Bible, particularly Genesis, report historical fact, or is it just a bunch of stories culled from other ancient cultures?
2. What does it mean for other cultures to have an influence on the Bible that we believe is revealed by God? Can we say that the Bible is unique or special? If the Bible is such a "culturally conditioned" product, what possible relevance can it have for us today?

3. Does this mean that the history of the church, which carried on for many centuries before this evidence came to light, was wrong in how it thought about its Bible?

These are some of the questions that Christians have been asking for the last several generations since ancient Near Eastern evidence first began coming to light. There are many ways of asking these questions, but they all boil down to this:

Is the Bible still the word of God?

Below I group into three headings the ten texts that we looked at above. These three headings reflect the kinds of problems that these texts raise for contemporary Christians and their understanding of the Bible. In this section, we will simply isolate these problems. In the following sections, we will look at how to address them.

1. Creation and the flood: *Enuma Elish*, *Atrahasis*, and *Gilgamesh*
2. Customs, laws, and proverbs: Nuzi documents, *Code of Hammurabi*, Hittite suzerain treaties, and *Instruction of Amenemope*
3. Israel and her kings: Tel Dan Inscription, Siloam Tunnel Inscription, and Mesha Inscription

Group 1—Creation and the Flood: Is Genesis Myth or History?

My intention is not to argue precisely where and how the Akkadian texts—*Enuma Elish*, *Atrahasis*, and *Gilgamesh*—parallel the biblical accounts. This is done too often, and it is typically done on the basis of an assumption that I very much call into question, namely, that the *more* Genesis looks like the Akkadian texts, the *less* inspired it is. Critical scholars tend to augment the similarities, even going beyond what has been warranted, and draw the general conclusion that Genesis is fundamentally no different from other ancient stories. On the other hand, conservative Christian scholars, particularly early on, have tended to employ a strategy of selective engagement of the evidence: highlighting extrabiblical evidence that conforms to or supports traditional views of the Bible, while either ignoring, downplaying, or arguing against evidence to the contrary. Regardless, *both* sides of the debate recognize that there is *some* relationship between the Akkadian texts and their biblical counterparts. If we can properly define the nature of that relationship, debates about the *implications* of that relationship will fall into place. Moving toward that goal is largely the point of this chapter.

The problem raised by these Akkadian texts is whether the biblical stories are historical: how can we say logically that the biblical stories are true and the Akkadian stories are false when they both look so very much alike? It is a common position among many modern scholars and biblically educated people that the ancient Near Eastern creation and flood stories are myth. This has led to the suggestion that the biblical story of creation is *every bit* as fanciful and unhistorical as the ancient Near Eastern stories.

Christians recoil from any suggestion that Genesis is in any way embedded in the mythologies of the ancient world. On one level this is understandable. After all, if the Bible and the gospel are true, and if that truth is bound up with historical events, you can't have the beginning of the Bible get it so wrong. It is important to understand, however, that not all historians of the ancient Near East use the word *myth* simply as shorthand for "untrue," "made-up," "storybook." It may include these ideas for some, but many who use the term are trying to get at something deeper. A more generous way of defining myth is that it is *an ancient, premodern, prescientific way of addressing questions of ultimate origins and meaning in the form of stories: Who are we? Where do we come from?*

Ancient peoples were not concerned to describe the universe in scientific terms. In fact, to put the matter more strongly: scientific investigation was not at the disposal of ancient Near Eastern peoples. Imagine yourself as a Mesopotamian, living perhaps one thousand to two thousand years before Abraham. There is virtually no communication with those outside your immediate location. There are no mass media. The light you have is from the sun, moon, campfire, and perhaps lamps. You are a simple hunter or herder, working each day so you can live another.

The scientific world in which we live and that we take so much for granted was inconceivable to ancient Mesopotamians. But ancient peoples, perhaps more contemplative than we are today, owing to the simplicity and rigor of their lives, wonder how it is that things are the way they are. Where does the sun go at night—or how did it get up there to begin with, and what keeps it from falling down like everything else does that gets tossed up in the air? Why are there seasons? Why does the moon move across the sky? Where does rain come from, and why does it seem to not be there when we need it most? Why do things grow out of the ground? Why do some animals feed off others? How did all we see around us begin? Of course, not everyone went through this questioning process, but they lived within traditions that had already provided some answers.

Ancient peoples composed lengthy stories to address these types of questions, and on some level the cause was attributed to unknown, powerful figures. It is impossible to know when the stories of the gods arose, but they did. I like to think that the imprint of God is so strong on his creation that, even apart from any knowledge of the true God, ancient peoples just knew that how and why they were here can be explained only by looking outside themselves. (They could teach modern people a thing or two!) So, stories were made up that aimed at answering questions of ultimate meaning. And one way of getting at these kinds of questions was by telling stories about the creation.

But this leads to a big problem for Christians today and their Bible. If the ancient Near Eastern stories are myth (defined in this way as prescientific stories of origins), and since the biblical stories are similar enough to these stories to invite comparison, does this indicate that myth is the proper category for understanding Genesis? Before the discovery of the Akkadian stories, one could quite safely steer clear of such a question, but this is no longer the case. We live in a modern world where we have certain expectations of how the world works. We neither understand the ancient ways—nor feel that we need to.

To give a hint of where this discussion is going, it is worth asking what standards we can reasonably expect of the Bible, seeing that it is an ancient Near Eastern document and not a modern one. Are the early stories in the Old Testament to be judged on the basis of standards of modern historical inquiry and scientific precision, things that ancient peoples were not at all aware of? Is it not likely that God would have allowed his word to come to the ancient Israelites according to standards *they* understood, or are modern standards of truth and error so universal that we should expect premodern cultures to have understood them? The former position is, I feel, better suited for solving the problem. The latter is often an implicit assumption of modern thinkers, *both conservative and liberal Christians*, but it is somewhat myopic and should be called into question. What the Bible is must be understood in light of the cultural context in which it was given.

Group 2—Customs, Laws, and Proverbs: Is Revelation Unique?

What makes the second group different from the first is that the ancient Near Eastern parallels seen in the Nuzi documents, *Code of Hammurabi*, Hittite suzerain treaties, and *Instruction of Amenemope* do not raise the specter of myth or legend. This is particularly the case with the Nuzi texts. The conclusion to be drawn from these texts is that the stories of Israel's first ancestors likely reach back to at least the middle of the second millennium BC. It is also true that the biblical stories were likely recorded in their present form sometime in the first millennium, since (1) Hebrew did not develop until late in the second millennium (more below), and (2) the stories of Israel's early ancestors contain many well-known anachronisms, particularly the references to the **Philistines**, who do not arrive on the scene until several hundred years after the time of Abraham, Isaac, and Jacob. Nevertheless, the Nuzi parallels can be called upon to provide a basic historical backdrop for the biblical accounts of Israel's early ancestors.

The issue that these texts raise, however, is the "moral situatedness" of the Old Testament. The moral standards by which Israel's first ancestors were expected to act seem to come not so much by God's unique command but by expectations of the surrounding cultures. The behavior of Israel's ancestors is not a matter of direct revelation by God, but of the accepted *cultural norms of the day*.

This point is even more problematic with respect to the law of Moses and the Proverbs of Solomon. Here we have explicit biblical laws and directives. And in the case of the former, these are given to Israel by God *directly* in what is arguably the foundational moment in Israel's entire history: the revelation of the law on Mount Sinai (Exod. 19–23). By anyone's dating of the life of Moses (the early **date of the exodus** is 1446 BC, the late date is 1280 BC), the *Code of Hammurabi* was still written several hundred years before the revelation of the law to Moses on Mount Sinai. In the case of Proverbs, although it is not described in the terms of a onetime revelation to Solomon, it nevertheless claims to be wisdom from God. It is precisely with respect to the *uniqueness* of Israel's law and wisdom, which seems to be presumed by the Bible itself at least with respect to the law, that the ancient Near Eastern parallels can become somewhat disconcerting.

To bring the issue into sharper focus, the problem really turns on what revelation means. What seems to be falsely implicit in the discussion is that revelation is by its nature unique, meaning that revelation will *necessarily* be *thoroughly* distinct from the surrounding culture. After all, it is thought, revelation is from God, but culture is a human product. But this is precisely the assumption that the ancient Near Eastern evidence forces us to look at more carefully. And this evidence indicates that (1) portions of the law and wisdom in the Old Testament have clear parallels in other ancient cultures, (2) those ancient Near Eastern parallels are *older* than their Old Testament counterparts, and (3) at least one of those parallels (*Amenemope*) seems to be the source for the biblical material.

In other words, the Bible seems to be relativized. It appears to be just another text from another ancient people, this one called "Israel." If ancient Mesopotamian and Egyptian literature have no claim on our lives today, why should Israelite literature be afforded that special status? The response might be, "Because it is Scripture and that makes it unique." The counterargument would be, "It's not unique in any recognizable way. Just look at the parallels." And so the argument goes. What needs to be called into question is the assumption that *both* sides of the argument are making, namely, that the situated/enculturated nature of the Bible poses a problem to the definition of divine revelation.

Group 3—Israel and Its Kings: Is Good Historiography Objective or Biased?

The texts in the third group—the inscriptions from Tel Dan, the Siloam Tunnel, and Mesha—are different still. These lend clear support to the basic historicity of the period of Israel's history typically referred to as the monarchic period, roughly from 1000 BC to 600 BC. As such, these texts do not create a problem to be solved. In fact, they could be called upon to address the kinds of problems we have seen in the first two groups of texts. Since these texts can be used to conclude that the historical period covered by 1–2 Samuel and 1–2 Kings (1–2 Chronicles is a different issue altogether and will come into play later in this chapter) is recorded with a degree of accuracy more in keeping with contemporary standards, can we not also conclude that the same can be said for Genesis and other early portions of the Bible?

This is a weak argument. First, to make an obvious point, the type of extrabiblical evidence we have for the monarchic period simply does not exist for the so-called primeval history (Gen. 1–11) and the long premonarchic period covered from Genesis 12 (beginning of the Abraham story) to the end of the period of the judges. It is questionable logic to reason backward from the historical character of the monarchic account, *for which there is some evidence*, to the primeval and ancestral stories, *for which such evidence is lacking*.

Second, at least one of the reasons why we have certain types of extrabiblical evidence from the monarchic period is that this was the period of relative stability and settledness for the Israelites. Israel was now a *nation* with its own king, palace, court, priests, temple, and many other institutions that other nations had. And, like other nations, Israel recorded in writing the events of its own kingdom. Some of these records are even mentioned in the Bible. To give just two examples:

> As for the other events of Solomon's reign—all he did and the wisdom he displayed—are they not written in the book of the annals of Solomon? (1 Kings 11:41)

> The other events of Jeroboam's reign, his wars and how he ruled, are written in the book of the annals of the kings of Israel. (1 Kings 14:19)

One would expect a more accurate, blow-by-blow account of Israel's history during this monarchic period, when it began to develop a more "historical self-consciousness," as it were. It is precisely the evidence *missing* from the previous periods of Israel's history that raises the problem of the essential historicity of that period.

So, in one respect, we are on somewhat firmer ground when we come to the monarchic period because it is there that we see something more closely resembling what one would expect of "good" history writing by modern standards: a more or less contemporary, eyewitness account. The Tel Dan and Siloam Tunnel inscriptions, although brief, are significant. They bear witness to the historicity of the reign of David and his descendants and the role that Hezekiah played in building the tunnel in the face of Sennacherib's military campaign.

But the Mesha Inscription raises another issue. This inscription is not a passing nod to the reign of an Israelite king (as is Tel Dan). It is itself a sustained literary product. It is an account of the reign of King Mesha of Moab, and, in a word, it is a seriously *biased* account of Mesha's reign. He can do no wrong. He does record a brief period of trouble with King Omri of Israel, but that is quickly taken care of because his god Chemosh came to the rescue. Other elements in the Mesha Inscription make it quite clear that this is not objective history writing, but history writing with an agenda, with an ax to grind, specifically, "I, King Mesha, am great."

The biblical accounts of the reigns of Israel's kings are different from other literature of the time in at least two respects. First, they are generally longer and therefore give a fuller picture. Second, and more importantly, the accounts of Israel's kings tend toward negative assessments. In fact, of the forty kings (twenty [counting Tibni, 1 Kings 16:21–22] from the **northern kingdom** and twenty from the **southern kingdom**) only one southern king (Josiah) is given an unqualified positive evaluation, while some others (namely, Hezekiah) are given slightly lesser but still positive evaluations. Northern kings are given consistently negative evaluations.

On the one hand, the willingness of the biblical writer(s) to criticize kings may suggest a degree of objectivity and sobriety on their part, which could imply greater historical accuracy. On the other hand, one may raise the question whether the histories recorded in 1–2 Samuel and 1–2 Kings might also be written from a certain perspective precisely because only *one southern king* receives nothing but praise. In other words, the Mesha Inscription raises the following problem: do biblical authors have an ax to grind as well? This suggestion will strike some as immediately suspect. If anything, would we not expect the Bible, which records God's revelation, to "get it right" by *not* allowing authors to be biased like all the other histories of the surrounding cultures, but instead just giving us the objective and neutral facts? No evangelical can consider this issue and not feel the force of this argument. If the Bible does not tell us what actually happened, how can we trust it about anything? Simply put, the problem before us is the historical character of precisely those Old Testament narratives that seem to report historical events.

To anticipate our discussion below, the questions we must ask are these: What were the *ancient* conventions for writing history? What did it mean to record history? What can be called good or accurate history writing by standards that were in existence when the Bible was written? In fact, one must question the entire assumption that good history writing, whether modern or ancient, is concerned to transmit *only* bare facts of history. Is there really any such thing as a completely objective and unbiased recording of history, modern or premodern?

How Have These Issues Been Handled in the Past?

The ancient Near Eastern evidence that began coming to light in the latter part of the nineteenth and the beginning of the twentieth centuries caught the church off guard. Until the nineteenth century the active issues for modern scholarship were largely textual, attempting to uncover the original form of the biblical text. After all, the Bible was two thousand to three thousand years old. Many copies and translations had been made, and in the course of copying and recopying and translating the Bible, errors crept in. Biblical scholars were engaged in trying to establish the original form of the Bible amid the myriad of copies. But with the increasing influence of ancient Near Eastern evidence, the questions began to include more directly the *setting* in which these texts were written, be it religious, political, cultural, or social. In other words, the issue began to shift from, "What did the *original documents* look like?" to, "What did the documents mean in their *original contexts*?"

It is fairly safe to say that a large impetus for investigating such questions about the Old Testament's ancient Near Eastern setting came from scholars who felt the need to bring Scripture into conversation with this mounting evidence. If the Bible is a historical document, then connecting it to its ancient settings is both inevitable and indispensable. Making such connections has proved to be extremely helpful. One need only open a modern study Bible to see the immediate impact that modern biblical scholarship has had on the church's understandings of Scripture. For example, the footnotes to Genesis in the *New International Version Study Bible* are dotted with references to ancient Near Eastern documents and customs to elucidate the biblical text.

For many, however, these findings come into direct conflict with church tradition. Many aspects of the Bible's ancient Near Eastern setting seem to poke large holes in what had been time-honored notions of the uniqueness of Scripture. Protestant church tradition developed over several centuries when Christians were not yet forced, by virtue of the culminating evidence, to see the Bible in its ancient context. Modern scholarship, in emphasizing the ancient context, sometimes dislodged the Bible from the church and its traditions. This was especially threatening in that some nineteenth-century scholars seemed bent on attacking the Bible. The conservative response, quite understandable given the tone of the time, was to defend the Bible. Both sides felt passionate about their own views, battle lines were drawn, and little constructive dialogue ensued. What may have been lost in the interchange was a constructive engagement of this new evidence by Christians with a high and healthy view of Scripture as God's word. And so we have a debate that is still very much an active issue, even though the battle lines shift from time to time.

How did biblical scholars of the nineteenth and twentieth centuries approach some of the issues outlined above? Many of the ancient texts listed above had the cumulative effect of casting serious doubt on the Bible's uniqueness vis-à-vis the ancient Near Eastern literature and the effects of this for revelation and inspiration. Also at stake were the related issues of historical accuracy, both with respect to the presence of ancient Near Eastern mythic parallels and the biased accounts of history in royal texts such as the Mesha Inscription. The end product of how modern biblical scholarship handled this new evidence was to present the Bible as more or less a purely human book. Sure, God (for those who even addressed the issue) can "speak" in the Bible—perhaps in the faraway echo of human voices expressing their ancient faith. But that is nothing like the traditional notion that God speaks to the church through time in these words. What modern biblical scholarship demonstrated was that the Bible shared many of the standards, concepts, and worldviews of its ancient Near Eastern neighbors. When they got down to it, there really wasn't anything about the Bible itself that made it all that special, and this seemed very inconsistent with conventional notions of inspiration and God speaking to us in the Bible today.

The newfound evidence for the cultural settings of the Bible led many to conclude that the Bible is *essentially* defined by these cultural factors. The "context of Scripture" became the *primary* determining factor in defining what the Bible is. That point of view had immediate doctrinal implications for evangelicals, irrespective of the fact that these implications were not always articulated by these scholars.

The conservatives' reaction was also problematic in that it implicitly assumed what their opponents also assumed: the Bible, being the word of God, ought to be historically accurate in all its details (since God would not lie or make errors) and unique in its own setting (since God's word is revealed, which implies a specific type of uniqueness). Rather than challenging these assumptions on a fundamental level, evangelicals adopted them, and so reaction was often intense. As mentioned earlier, conservatives have tended to employ a strategy of selective engagement, embracing evidence that seems to support their assumptions (such as might be done with Tel Dan and the Siloam Tunnel) but retreating from evidence that seems to undercut these assumptions (e.g., *Enuma Elish*, *Code of Hammurabi*). In other words, conservative scholarship, allowing modern scholarship to set the agenda while still trying to maintain older doctrinal commitments, was well positioned to listen to some evidence but not all.

To caricature somewhat, if historical context was everything for liberal scholars, regardless of its implications for Christian doctrine, for conservative scholars doctrine was everything, regardless of the historical evidence that challenged doctrine. This impasse defined much of the scholarly landscape for decades. Though there was an impasse, it is inaccurate to say that it was a complete stalemate. Theories that once defined older liberalism gave way to newer theories. Also, there has been movement among evangelical scholars in that many routinely employ a variety of methods and draw certain conclusions that in previous generations were highly suspect.

Such a thing is inevitable, but the *doctrinal implications of the Bible being so much a part of its ancient contexts* are still not being addressed as much as they should. Many evangelical scholars do excellent historical work but do not always squarely address the doctrinal implications of their own findings. More than once, I have observed evangelical scholars pursue a line of argumentation about Genesis or some other topic, come close to drawing out the logical implications for how we understand the Bible, but then retreat to traditional, safe categories. Likewise, and perhaps more commonly, problematic evidence is simply ignored or dismissed in an effort to protect the Bible (or better, one's beliefs about how the Bible should be). Even worse, simplistic and irresponsible arguments are sometimes mounted that serve no purpose other than to affirm established positions.

Such a posture is an intellectual curiosity for those outside evangelicalism. But to those who struggle to synthesize their own doctrinal commitments with what we have learned about the Bible over the past 150 years, these ways of handling the evidence can be both frustrating and even debilitating.

How Can We Think Differently through These Issues?

As I attempt to move beyond this impasse in my own thinking, I find that the issue is not to be engaged purely on the level of evidence. To be sure, this chapter is largely about the significance of evidence, which must be engaged with both enthusiasm and patience. The heart of the matter, however, is not the latest archeological find to prove (or disprove) the Bible. As I see it, the issue concerns the assumptions made *by both sides* of the debate about *how to understand that evidence*. In other words, the assumptions we have about the nature of God (which includes notions of revelation and inspiration), what constitutes reality, what is good history writing, and so on, will largely determine *how* we understand the evidence. My intention below is to explore how the biblical and extrabiblical evidence can affect these assumptions. If, in full conversation with the biblical and extrabiblical evidence, we can *adjust our expectations* about how the Bible should behave, we can begin to move beyond the impasse of the liberal/conservative debates of the last several generations.

Toward that end, I wish to make clear two assumptions that will be important in what follows:

1. I assume that the extrabiblical archeological and textual evidences should play an important role in our understanding of Scripture. Ours is a historical faith, and to uproot the Bible from its historical contexts is self-contradictory. In and of themselves, these evidences are not wholly *determinative*; some are clearer and more relevant than others. They must be looked at carefully and patiently and thus interpreted as to their importance. Though they are not determinative, they are wholly relevant to how we understand today what the Bible *is*. To state the opposite, I reject the notion that a modern doctrine of Scripture can be articulated in blissful isolation from the evidence we have.
2. All attempts to articulate the nature of Scripture are open to examination, including my own. I firmly believe—although it

may seem somewhat paradoxical—that the Spirit of God is fully engaged in such a theological process *and at the same time* that our attempts to articulate what God's word is have a necessarily provisional dimension. To put it succinctly: the Spirit *leads* the church to truth—he does not simply drop us down in the middle of it. To say this is not a low view of Scripture or of the role of the Holy Spirit. It is simply to recognize what has been the case throughout the history of the church, that diverse views and changes of opinion over time have been the constant companions of the church and that God has not brought this process to a closure.

The findings of the past 150 years have made extrabiblical evidence an unavoidable conversation partner. The result is that, as perhaps never before in the history of the church, we can see how truly provisional and incomplete certain dimensions of our understanding of Scripture can be. On the other hand, we are encouraged to encounter the depth and riches of God's revelation and to rely more and more on God's Spirit, who speaks to the church in Scripture.

Is Genesis Myth or History?

The parallels between the opening chapters of Genesis and *Enuma Elish* and *Atrahasis/Gilgamesh* raise the issue whether there is myth in the Old Testament. This has certainly been a pressing issue among evangelicals, for, if Genesis is myth, it seems to bring the Bible down to the level of other ancient literature.

Taking the extrabiblical evidence into account, I question how much value there is in posing the choice of Genesis as either myth or history. This distinction seems to be a modern invention. It presupposes—without stating explicitly—that what is historical, in a modern sense of the word, is more real, of more value, more like something God would do, than myth. So, the argument goes, if Genesis is myth, then it is not "of God." Conversely, if Genesis is history, only then is it something worthy of the name "Bible." Again, it is interesting to me that both sides of the liberal/conservative debate share at least to a certain extent these kinds of assumptions. The liberal might answer, "Yes, it is myth, and this proves it is not inspired, and who cares anyway?" The conservative might answer, "Well, since we know that the Bible is God's word, we know it can't be myth." And so great effort is expended to drive as much distance as possible between the Bible and any ancient Near Eastern literature that poses problems.

But one might ask *why* it is that God *can't* use the category *we* call "myth" to speak to *ancient* Israelites. We seem to think of myth as something ancient people thought up because they didn't want to listen to what God said, and so at the outset of the discussion the Bible is already set up in *full contrast* to the ancient Near Eastern literature. I don't think this is the case. If some consensus could be reached for an alternative term, it would seem profitable to abandon the word *myth* altogether, since the term has such a long history of meanings attached to it, which prejudices the discussion from the outset. There is no consensus for another word, so, before we proceed, allow me to repeat how I use the word *myth* in the discussion below: *Myth is an ancient, premodern, prescientific way of addressing questions of ultimate origins and meaning in the form of stories: Who are we? Where do we come from?*

We must begin our thinking by acknowledging that the ancient Near Eastern myths are almost certainly older than the versions recorded for us in the Bible. How can we say this? For several reasons.

First, Israelite culture is somewhat of a latecomer in the ancient Near Eastern world. This is not to deny the antiquity of such figures as Abraham, Isaac, and Jacob, for example, or the stories surrounding them. But even this most ancient era of Israel's history is much more recent than the Sumerian, Akkadian, and Egyptian cultures that formed the backdrop of Israel's world.

Second, the culture of Israel's ancestors was certainly oral; writing was generally restricted to established, settled kingdoms and was not found among wandering peoples. We must remember that there were no "books" as we know them today. We can easily pick up our Bibles and read them or move them from place to place. The codex, however, a forerunner of the modern book, was not developed until the first century BC. In the second millennium, if any permanence was desired, writing was either etched in stone or pressed into large blocks of wet clay. Egyptian writing on papyrus scrolls is also a documented practice, but not one that would have been employed by common people. It is safe to assume that Israel's ancient stories were composed first orally in the context of the well-established ancient Near Eastern cultures of the day and were committed to writing only at a later time. It is unlikely that wanderers like Abraham or Israelite slaves would have had in their possession either numerous papyrus scrolls or the many (heavy!!) tablets needed to record the stories in Genesis. One wonders if a preoccupation with the written word would even have been a part of their thinking.

Third, the Hebrew language we know from the Old Testament did not exist in the second millennium. To be sure, linguistic "ancestors" of Biblical Hebrew were very much in existence during that time. Many scholars see reflexes of Hebrew-like elements in Akkadian and Egyptian texts from the first half of the second millennium BC. Such similarities certainly suggest Hebrew's clear connections to its Semitic predecessors. Ugaritic, for example, is a language very similar to Biblical Hebrew. We have texts from these ancient peoples that date to around 1400 BC and later.

But these factors do not directly affect the question of when the stories of Genesis came to be written in Hebrew. To attempt to answer this question, other factors must be thrown into the mix.

First, the Semitic alphabet, which formed the basis for not only Hebrew but also other Semitic languages (e.g., Aramaic, Moabite, Edomite, Ammonite)—not to mention the Greek and Latin alphabets—did not come on the scene until about 1700 BC and then only in a very rudimentary fashion, and it did not catch on right away. The invention of the alphabet, a far simpler writing system than that used for Sumerian and Akkadian, certainly contributed to the eventual spread of literacy, but this is far from saying that the proper conditions existed for the production of a sustained literary product like Genesis, written in Hebrew by a wandering and enslaved people in the middle portion of the second millennium. This is not to say that these stories did not already exist in oral form before they were written down; they were not "invented" at some later point. But these oral versions *already* reflected ancient worldviews. In other words, although the biblical stories existed earlier in oral form and only later were written down in Hebrew, one cannot argue that this oral prehistory insulated them from the influences of the ancient Near Eastern stories present in the surrounding cultures. Rather, it establishes a connection. The writing down of these stories later in the alphabetic language of Hebrew simply represents a time when the technological and sociological conditions were ready for such a development.

Second, we have no extrabiblical evidence for the existence of Hebrew before the first millennium BC. The earliest Hebrew text currently known to us from outside the Old Testament may be the **Gezer Calendar**, which dates to the tenth century BC. There is still some question, however, about whether it is written in Hebrew or in Phoenician, Hebrew's parent language. The text is fairly short (nineteen words), so there is not much to go on. The earliest biblical *manuscripts* are from the **Dead Sea Scrolls** and are no earlier than the second century BC. The relative lack of evidence does not mean that nothing like Hebrew existed before the first millennium. But the degree to which Hebrew or an early version of Hebrew existed even at the very end of the second millennium must remain an open question. Hence, to insist that someone living in the middle of the second millennium BC would have communicated the stories of Genesis in a language that was identical to the Hebrew known to us from the Old Testament is simply an assertion, one that runs counter to the linguistic evidence available to us. Again, it may be safe to assume that the stories of Genesis existed by this time, but the available evidence leads to the conclusion that they were not recorded in their present form until sometime in the first millennium. In both their oral and written versions, the stories of Genesis seem to be younger than the stories of other ancient Near Eastern cultures.

If pressed, one could attempt to mount the argument that the Israelite stories were actually older than all the ancient Near Eastern stories but were only *recorded* later in Hebrew. Such a theory—for that is what it is, a theory—would need to *assume* that the biblical stories are the pristine originals and that all the other stories are parodies and perversions of the Israelite original, even though the available evidence would be very difficult to square with such a conclusion. But could it have happened this way? Yes, I suppose one could insist on such a thing, but it would be very difficult for someone holding to such a view to have a meaningful conversation with linguists and historians of the ancient world. To argue in such hypothetical terms can sometimes become an excuse for maintaining a way of thinking that is otherwise unsupportable. It is just such explanations that some readers might find problematic, for they seem motivated by a desire to protect one's theology rather than to engage the available evidence.

Despite what has been said about the origins of Hebrew, we still have not squarely addressed the most fundamental issue: regardless of when Genesis was written and in what language, it still reflects an ancient Near Eastern worldview that clearly is significantly older. It stretches logic and common sense to try to protect the uniqueness of the Genesis accounts by arguing that Mesopotamian peoples, who existed long before Israel came on the scene and who were the dominant cultures of the day, had no creation myths for hundreds of years and simply waited for Israelite slaves to provide the prototype, which they then corrupted.

So how is it that Genesis can look so much like other ancient Near Eastern texts? I propose a simple scenario that begins with Abraham. Here we have a story, beginning at the end of Genesis 11, about a resident of *Babylon* whose family left there and moved up along the Euphrates River to Haran (in modern-day Turkey). According to Genesis 12, God called Abraham out of his homeland. This is the biblical portrait of Israel's rise in history; it begins in Babylon. Relevant here, too, is Joshua 24:2:

> Joshua said to all the people, "This is what the LORD, the God of Israel, says: 'Long ago your forefathers, including Terah the father of Abraham and Nahor, *lived beyond the River and worshiped other gods.*'"

It is important to remember where Abraham came from and where he was headed. He was not an Israelite. There were no such people yet. He came from "Ur of the Chaldeans" (Gen. 15:7). Ur is actually a city of Sumerian origin, a culture even older than the Assyrian and Babylonian cultures we have looked at. *The Mesopotamian world from which Abraham came was one whose own stories of origins had been expressed in mythic categories for a considerable length of time. Moreover, the land Abraham was going to enter, the land of the Canaanites, was likewise rich in its own myths.*

Keeping in the forefront of our minds the biblical portrait of Israel's first father as an ancient Mesopotamian man may be a helpful starting point from which to understand the origin of Israel's creation story. As God entered into a relationship with Abraham, he "met" him where he was—an ancient Mesopotamian man who breathed the air of the ancient Near East. We must surely assume that Abraham, as such a man, shared the worldview of those whose world he shared and not a modern, scientific one. The reason the opening chapters of Genesis look so much like the literature of ancient Mesopotamia is that the worldview categories of the ancient Near East were ubiquitous and normative at the time. Of course, different cultures had different myths, but the point is that they all had them.

The reason the biblical account is different from its ancient Near Eastern counterparts is not that it is history in the modern sense of the word and therefore divorced from any similarity to ancient Near Eastern myth. What makes Genesis different from its ancient Near Eastern counterparts is that it begins to make the point to Abraham and his seed that the God they are bound to, the God who called them into existence, is different from the gods around them.

We might think that such a scenario is unsatisfying because it gives too much ground to pagan myths. But we must bear in mind how very *radical* this notion would have been in the ancient world. For a second-millennium Semitic people, as Israel's earliest ancestors were, to say that the gods of Babylon were not worth worshiping but that the true god was the god of a nomad like Abraham—this was risky, ridiculous, and counterintuitive. And this would have been no less true when these stories were later recorded in Hebrew. Ancient Near Eastern religions were hierarchical and polytheistic. The biblical claim that Israel's God, **Yahweh**, alone is God might be analogous to someone claiming in our world today that the gods of ancient Greece *really* exist and that they sit on Mount Olympus ruling the world.

To put it differently, God adopted Abraham as the forefather of a new people, and in doing so he also adopted the mythic categories within which Abraham—and everyone else—thought. But God did not simply

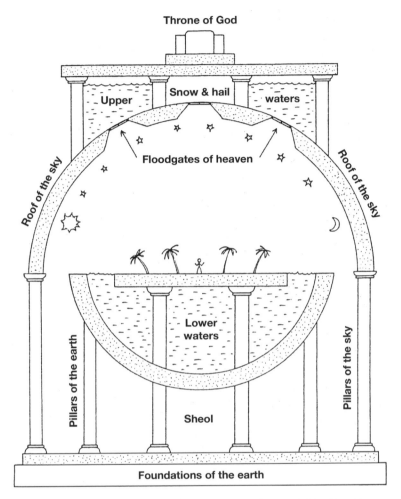

Biblical and ancient Near Eastern worldview. ***Source***: Alan P. Dickin, *On a Faraway Day . . . : A New View of Genesis in Ancient Mesopotamia* (Columbus, GA: Brentwood Christian Press, 2002), 122. Used by permission of the author.

leave Abraham in his mythic world. Rather, God *transformed* the ancient myths so that Israel's story would come to focus on its God, the real one.

Genesis—as other stories of the ancient world—thus portrays the world as a flat disk with a dome above. Below the earth were the waters threatening to gush up, and above the dome are the waters threatening to drop down (see Gen. 7:11). The biblical worldview described in Genesis is an ancient Near Eastern one. But the ordering of the world (e.g., the separation of water from land) did not result from a morbid conflict within a dysfunctional divine family, as we read in *Enuma Elish*. It was simply this amazing God who spoke.

I am assiduously avoiding any suggestion that Genesis borrows from the Babylonian stories in any direct way. As I mentioned earlier, the degree to which Genesis might have been dependent on the Babylonian material has always been a matter of debate, and there is no need to commit ourselves to one view or another. Some scholars argue, quite persuasively in fact, that the differences between Genesis and *Enuma Elish* are so great that one cannot speak of any *direct* relationship. I feel this is essentially correct (although the stronger similarities regarding the flood story may suggest some level of dependence). But again, the point here is not one of *textual* dependence but of *conceptual* similarity. The differences notwithstanding, the opening chapters of Genesis participate in a worldview that the earliest Israelites shared with their Mesopotamian neighbors. To put it this way is not to concede ground to liberalism or unbelief, but to understand the simple fact that the stories in Genesis had a context within which they were first understood. And that context was not a modern scientific one but an ancient mythic one.

The biblical account, along with its ancient Near Eastern counterparts, assumes the factual nature of what it reports. They did not think, "We know this is all 'myth' but it will have to do until science is invented to give us better answers." We do not protect the Bible or render it more believable to modern people by trying to demonstrate that it is consistent with modern science. In the ancient context, which existed thousands of years before modern science came on the scene, the Bible needed no such defense. And, in its original setting, the Bible was already a radical challenge to the status quo.

Therefore, the question is not the degree to which Genesis conforms to what we would think is a proper description of origins. It is a fundamental misunderstanding of Genesis to expect it to answer questions generated by a modern worldview, such as whether the days were literal or figurative, or whether the days of creation can be lined up with modern science, or whether the flood was local or universal. The question that Genesis is prepared to answer is whether Yahweh, the God of Israel, is worthy of worship. And that point is made not by allowing ancient Israelites to catch a glimpse of a spherical earth or a heliocentric universe. It is wholly incomprehensible to think that thousands of years ago God would have felt constrained to speak in a way that would be meaningful only to Westerners several thousand years later. To do so borders on modern, Western arrogance. Rather, Genesis makes its case in a way that ancient men and women would have readily understood—indeed, the *only* way.

To argue, as I am doing here, that such biblical stories as creation and the flood must be understood first and foremost in the ancient contexts, is nothing new. The point I would like to emphasize, however, is that such a firm grounding in ancient myth does not make Genesis less inspired; it is not a concession that we must put up with or an embarrassment to a sound doctrine of Scripture. Quite to the contrary, such rootedness in the culture of the time is precisely what it means for God to speak to his people.

This is what it means for God to speak at a certain time and place—he enters *their* world. He speaks and acts in ways that make sense to *them*. This is surely what it means for God to reveal himself to people—he accommodates, condescends, meets them where they are. The phrase *word of God* does not imply disconnectedness to its environment. In fact, if we can learn a lesson from the incarnation of God in Christ, it demands the exact opposite. And if God was willing and ready to adopt an ancient way of thinking, we truly hold a very low view of Scripture indeed if we make that into a point of embarrassment. We will not understand the Bible if we push aside or explain away its cultural setting, even if that setting disturbs us. We should, rather, learn to be thankful that God came to them just as he did more fully in Bethlehem many, many centuries later. We must resist the notion that for God to enculturate himself is somehow beneath him. This is precisely how he shows his love to the world he made.

Is Revelation Unique?

Our second group of texts (Nuzi documents, Hittite suzerainty treaties, *Code of Hammurabi*, *Instruction of Amenemope*) demonstrates that ancient Israelite customs and ethical standards (laws and proverbs) are not absolutely unique to Israel. To put it more specifically, what marks off Israel's legal and wisdom texts is not the unique *content* of these texts; it is something else. Sure, Israel's ethical standards are its own and there are elements unique to it. But on the whole, Israel's collection of law and wisdom demonstrates that the Israelites were well at home in the ancient Semitic world. Whatever differences exist are striking only because of the fundamental similarities.

The importance of the Nuzi documents differs from that of the others in the second group. Strictly speaking, when Abraham fathers a child with Hagar, he is not doing so in response to a revelatory command from God. He is simply following Sarah's advice, which is precisely what Genesis says and which, according to the Nuzi documents, had cultural support. The same holds for the other examples mentioned above. There is no claim being made here that the social customs of Israel's first ancestors are the result of God's unique intrusion into human affairs, no command of God announcing that a man must father a child with his wife's handmaiden. However indelicate such a family dynamic may appear to us, the point is simply this: what constituted Israel's proper social—and, in this case, even ethical—behavior seems to be a matter of cultural convention. There is no suggestion in Genesis that these social customs are there by God's design and *that* is what makes them "okay." These customs were simply there, before Abraham came on the scene.

When we move to the topics of law and proverbs, we see much of the same thing. Even though Israel's law was revealed by God through Moses on Mount Sinai, these laws were by no means unique to them. It is hard to imagine that, until Mount Sinai, neither the Israelites nor the surrounding ancient Near Eastern nations had any idea that murder was wrong (the story of Cain and Abel, regardless of when it was written, assumes a knowledge that murder is wrong long before Mount Sinai), or that one should honor one's parents or that giving false testimony about another is a great offense. What makes Israel's laws revelatory is not that they are new—a moral about-face vis-à-vis the surrounding nations—but that *these* are the laws that were to be obeyed in order to form Israel into a godlike community.

If anything is unique about Israel's law, it is how that law is introduced (Exod. 20:1–6):

> And God spoke all these words:
> "I am the LORD your God, who brought you out of Egypt, out of the land of slavery.
> "You shall have no other gods before me.
> "You shall not make for yourself an idol in the form of anything in heaven above or on the earth beneath or in the waters below. You shall not bow down to them or worship them; for I, the LORD your God, am a jealous God, punishing the children for the sin of the fathers to the third and fourth generation of those who hate me, but showing love to a thousand generations of those who love me and keep my commandments."

Exodus 20:2 is the preamble to the Ten Commandments and lays out the reason why Israel should be faithful to God (as we saw with the Hittite treaties mentioned earlier): God acted in history *to bring the Israelites out of Egypt*. This is what he did. What is now expected of Israel is to obey. Exodus 20:3–6 contains the first two commandments, a sort of one-two punch that accents Israel's uniqueness over against the nations: (1) Yahweh is Israel's only God; (2) Israel should not worship any god (whether Yahweh or false gods) in the form of some created thing, an

idol. It is these two commandments that set Israel on a collision course
with its neighbors: they all had multiple gods, and the worship of gods
by means of idols was as common as going to church on Sunday is for
us today.

The motivation and historical conditions of Israel's law code are very
different from its neighbors. But when you look at specific laws, the
degree of similarity is obvious. Systems of sacrifice and priestly rituals
were common to all ancient Near Eastern religions before, during, and
after Israel's laws were enacted. And, as we saw above, biblical laws and
ancient Near Eastern law codes cover very similar situations in similar
wording: false accusations, stealing, stolen property, kidnapping, treatment of slaves, livestock, land, loans, marriage and divorce, children,
and so on. It is no exaggeration to say that anyone familiar with ancient
Near Eastern law codes, reading biblical law for the first time, although
likely taking note of elements peculiar to the Israelites, would no doubt
recognize it as "another ancient Near Eastern law code."

The same holds for the book of Proverbs, perhaps even more so.
Proverbs makes no claim that its contents are revealed to Israel through
some special event, such as is the case with the law. Rather, it is a body
of sayings, many of which are readily affirmed by common sense (hold
your tongue, don't be greedy) and that find ample parallels in the wisdom literature of the ancient Near East. But despite the common, even
secular feel (as some put it) to Proverbs, it is at the same time a book
that claims that, in following the path of wisdom laid out therein, one
is connecting with *God's* wisdom. Although the specific content of Proverbs may seem more or less commonplace, we see something similar to
what we have seen with respect to law: what is common is used by God
for a special purpose. To put it another way, God's law and wisdom are
incarnated in the world of the ancient Near East: they fit.

What makes Proverbs revelatory is not its uniqueness over against
its ancient Near Eastern environment, nor is it because it was specially
dispensed at one point in time to the Israelites and to the Israelites only,
so that any similarity to other wisdom texts is due to their borrowing
Israel's wisdom texts. Rather, what we have with both law and wisdom
is a way of behaving that may precede any written codes of conduct.
Perhaps it is the case that what we find in Exodus and Proverbs, the *Code
of Hammurabi* and the *Instruction of Amenemope*, and others, reflects a
deeper reality, that God has set up the world in a certain way and that
way is imprinted on all people. When Israel, therefore, produces a body
of law and wisdom, it is not to say, "Look at this new thing we have that
no one else has." Instead it is the author of *all law and wisdom* bringing
a certain standard of conduct to bear upon Israel in order to make them

into a certain kind of people—a people who embody the character of God to a world that did not recognize him.

What will become immediately apparent to any careful reader of Israel's law and wisdom literature is that there is a fair amount of diversity. The laws of Exodus and Deuteronomy are not exactly the same, even where they treat similar subjects; proverbs that cover the same topic say different things. We will look at this in more detail in chapter 3. For now the only point I wish to make is that our second group of texts has a direct bearing on how we understand the Bible. What makes Israel's law and wisdom literature unique is not so much *what* it says (although that is certainly true with various laws), but Israel's claim to be connected to the one true God who alone has the right to lay these claims upon them. That is the message to the other nations: *This is the law of God who delivered us from Egypt; this is the wisdom of God who created heaven and earth. We worship him.* The similarities between Israel's conduct and that of the other nations does not make Israel less unique among the nations any more than Jesus' sharing in the customs and practices of first-century Palestine makes him less unique. Rather, both Israel's practices and Christ himself are evidence of "God with us."

Is Good Historiography Objective or Biased?

Our third group of texts (the Mesha, Tel Dan, and Siloam Tunnel inscriptions) affects our understanding of Israel's history writing (historiography). These are by no means the only such texts, nor are they even the most important ones; they are just representative of the whole.

This issue is a bit different from the other two discussed in this chapter. The problem of Old Testament historiography is not one generated solely by the ancient Near Eastern evidence, however relevant it may be. Rather, it is a problem internal to the Old Testament itself. We see this most clearly when we compare 1–2 Chronicles with 1–2 Samuel and 1–2 Kings: both cover much of the same period of Israel's history (the rise and fall of Israel's monarchy), but they tell that history in markedly different ways. Thus, not only the extrabiblical evidence but the *Bible itself* force us to think very carefully about what we should expect of the Bible as a historical document. This has been a major concern of evangelicalism, especially as it attempted to respond to the attacks of modern scholarship, which worked with both the biblical and extrabiblical evidence.

First, let's remind ourselves of the evidence from Tel Dan and the Siloam Tunnel. Both of these ancient texts make a *passing reference* to something we find in the Old Testament: David's descendants and

Hezekiah's tunnel. As such they remind us of the basic factual nature of the account of Israel's history as found in the Old Testament. I certainly do not want to draw too much from these examples, but, in my view, the basic historical character of Israel's monarchic period as described in the Old Testament cannot be seriously doubted.

But this does not help us very much with the topic before us here. A passing reference to a historical fact is just that, a passing reference. It is not historiography. Historiography is not the mere *statement* of facts but the *shaping* of these facts for a particular *purpose*. To put it another way, historiography is an attempt to relay to someone the *significance* of history.

For example, that I am staring out my window right now thinking about what to write next is a "historical fact." But you may rightly ask, "Who cares?" (apart from my publisher). Likewise, that I just got back from dropping my daughter Elizabeth off at swim practice in the pouring rain on a June morning is historically verifiable, but it is not historiography. We can move even further back in time. That Gandhi lived and fought for the independence of India from England is true, factual, free from error, historical, but that does not make it historiography. The 1982 movie about Gandhi starring Ben Kingsley, however, is most certainly historiography. What makes it so? It is a *sustained* attempt to capture the life of Gandhi in a *particular* way to *persuade* us of the *importance* and *significance* of Gandhi's life.

Again, the Tel Dan and Siloam Tunnel inscriptions are not historiography. They are simply witnesses (important ones) to historical events. The Mesha Inscription, however, is different. True, this inscription's passing mention of Omri is likewise a witness to historical fact, but the Mesha Inscription as a whole was not written for that purpose. Rather it is an argument that Mesha was a great king. In a word, the Mesha Inscription is propaganda. I hesitate to use this word because of its negative connotations. Nevertheless, this inscription is a biased account of the *significance* of Mesha's reign. In it Mesha brags of building a **high place** for the Moabite god Chemosh and that, by Chemosh's design (not to mention Mesha's effective rule), Israel "has gone to ruin for ever" (which did not happen). Whatever mistakes and blunders Mesha surely made during his reign do not enter the picture. The Mesha Inscription is by no means an isolated example of this in the ancient Semitic world. Rather, it is quite typical.

We noted earlier that Israel's accounts of the monarchic period differ in terms of their historical feel from what we read in Genesis and other books that pertain to events before the monarchic period. Many explain this difference by appealing to Israel's not becoming a settled, independent nation until the monarchic period, which put it in a better position to record its own history in a self-reflective manner. I am largely in agreement with this explanation, but this does not mean that Israel's historiography of the monarchic period is objective or unbiased. In fact, it is precisely *because* it represents Israel's *self-reflection* that it is "biased."

This can be demonstrated by looking at 1–2 Samuel and 1–2 Kings (Samuel–Kings), a collection of writings that takes us from the very beginning of Israel's monarchy (its first king, Saul) to the fall of the northern kingdom and finally to the fall of the southern kingdom. These writings are not the objective reporting of an insurance adjuster. They are historiography, and as such they contain three interrelated elements common to *any* historiography:

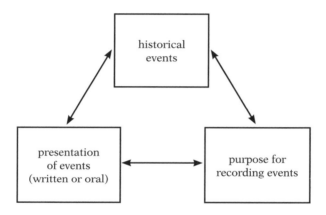

This diagram illustrates that there are indeed such things as historical *events*, and any attempt at historiography will necessarily interact with these events (although these events may be in the distant past and therefore mediated to the writer via a long tradition of understanding). And when one attempts to communicate the significance of those events, one is engaged in historiography. This is where *presentation* and *purpose* come in.

The two-way arrows indicate that these three elements continually have a mutual effect on each other. *All* historiography is a literary product, which means it is about people writing down (or transmitting orally) their *version* of that history. In other words, historiography is by definition an *interpretive* exercise. There might not be much that is interpretive about saying "David lived," but when you give an account of David's life—what he did, when, with whom, why, what the implications were—you are most certainly engaged in interpreting these events. How so? Anyone who communicates historical events must be very selective about what is communicated. You simply can't say *everything*, nor would you want to. You say only those things that are important to the point you want to get across. Also, you will say those things *in such a way* that will drive your point home. In other words, this presentation, this literary product, looks the way it does because the author has a purpose in mind for why those events should be reported. The presentation is not divorced from the events, but it is a purposeful representation of those events.

These three elements are always interconnected. All written accounts of history are *literary products* that are based on *historical events* that are shaped to conform to the *purpose* the historian wants to get across. This is true of the Mesha Inscription, and it is no less true of Samuel–Kings. This, too, is a literary product written for a purpose, which in the mind of most scholars appears to be an explanation for why Israel went into exile. The answer given in Samuel–Kings is the refrain that the kings persisted in practicing idolatry. We should remember that alternate histories of Israel *could* have been written from many different angles emphasizing many different episodes in Israel's history. But Samuel–Kings is what it is. That Israel's historiography is written for such a purpose does not make it untrue because it is not objective. It is simply an interpretation of the historical events designed for a special purpose, namely, "This is what brought us into exile."

I want to emphasize as strongly as possible that to explain the nature of historiography in Samuel–Kings this way is not to paint it in a negative light, as if it is bad historiography because it is biased. The truth of the matter is that *all* historiography exhibits the interplay between event, presentation, and purpose. To be direct, there is *no* historiography that does not have a decidedly interpretive element. Our understanding of the significance of world events may be affected by the written presentations of *Newsweek* or *Time*. They don't say the same things about the same events. Or watch the evening news: CNN, ABC, CBS, NBC, and FOX are all visual presentations (as opposed to the written word or still photos of news magazines), but they certainly differ from one another.

Portraits of the Civil War differ depending on who wrote them and when they lived. We can well imagine a late-nineteenth-century account of the Civil War by a Southern historian differing from a twenty-first-century account written by a German-born historian of American culture. We should not presume that the former is more biased because it is written by a Southerner. Neither would this account be more accurate simply because it is written closer to the time of the events. Likewise, the modern German version is not less biased because it is written by an objective German nor less accurate because so much time has transpired since the war itself. The fact is that *both* are biased: they were written by different people living in different times, places, and cultures and for different purposes.

This very same phenomenon of histories written from different per-spectives can be seen in the pages of the Bible itself, and this is where we must maintain an open mind to how Scripture behaves. In the Old Testament we indeed have *two differing* accounts of virtually the same historical period. Along with Samuel–Kings we also have 1–2 Chronicles, which, excluding the genealogies of 1 Chronicles 1–9, covers the same period: from the early days of the monarchy to the exile.

I venture to say that many of us skip over Chronicles or at least read it quickly. After all, coming as it does right after Samuel–Kings and covering much of the same ground, it can be tedious to read—especially if we are reading through the Old Testament in order. How many of us, having just read Samuel–Kings, feel we can safely skip over Chronicles, since we "just read that"—plus, Chronicles begins with nine chapters of names! Much of the blame for all this rests on the shoulders of the compilers of the Septuagint. In the Hebrew Old Testament, Chronicles is not tucked right after Samuel–Kings but is the *last* book of the Old Testament (the English canonical order is taken from the Septuagint, not the Hebrew order). Even the Greek name given to Chronicles in the Septuagint is a problem: "the things left over" (Greek *paraleipomenon*). I suspect many Christians read Chronicles in just this way, thinking of it as things left over from Samuel–Kings.

That Chronicles is last in the Hebrew canonical order indicates some-thing very important. Chronicles was probably not written merely to supplement Samuel–Kings. Rather it is an independent piece of histo-riography that, although certainly interacting with Samuel–Kings, is nevertheless intended to stand on its own and be understood on its own terms. It is not just that part of the Bible that can be safely skipped over in morning devotions in order to get to Ezra and Nehemiah. It tells an *alternate* history of Israel, one that differs from Samuel–Kings because it is told from *a different perspective and for different reasons*, namely, from the perspective of those who had returned from captivity in Babylon. (This occurred in 538 BC, and Chronicles was likely written sometime in the fifth or fourth century BC.)

We cannot overestimate the impact of Israel's exile. Samuel–Kings makes the emphatic point that a descendant of David will *never* cease sitting on the throne in Jerusalem (2 Sam. 7, which we will look at briefly below). But what happened? Israel went into exile, which meant no king, no temple, no sacrifice, no land. All of these things had been evidence of God's favor, but in one brief period of time (597–587 BC) the powerful Babylonians ended it all. So, what of God's promises? This is (among other things) what Chronicles addresses. And this is where the (boring) list of names in 1 Chronicles 1–9 comes in. Here we have a postexilic Israelite community trying to reconnect to God's promises. In doing so it traces its heritage back—way back—to Adam, which is the very first word in the book.

Chronicles is not interested in merely recounting past events for the sake of it. Rather the author is employing Israel's past for the purpose of interpreting its own *present* circumstances in terms of the broadest possible context. The author is reminding the people that despite their difficult present circumstances, they have a heritage that is long and honored. To put it another way, the returning exiles were asking whether they were still the people of God, whether his promises to them were still true. How can they still be God's people if all these promises have been dashed? Chronicles retells Israel's past in order to encourage the Israel of the present.

In the next chapter we will revisit Chronicles in the context of theological diversity. For now, by looking at one example, we can catch a glimpse of how Chronicles addresses these questions. In 2 Samuel 7:16, the prophet Nathan promises that David's descendants would still sit on the throne in Jerusalem forever:

> Your house and your king will endure forever before me; your throne will be established forever.

Chronicles reports this same exchange differently in 1 Chronicles 17:14:

> I will set him over my house and my kingdom forever; his throne will be established forever.

It is worth noting—to make the somewhat obvious point—that these two accounts report the same event (Nathan's words to David) in different ways. This is indicative of what we find throughout Chronicles' historiography—the author shapes the events to suit his theological purpose.

I want to focus on the first half of these verses. In 2 Samuel, Nathan is speaking to David and refers to "*your* house . . . *your* king"—meaning David's descendants. In Chronicles this becomes "*my* house . . . *my* kingdom." What is happening? In Samuel–Kings, Israel's future is centered on the perpetuation of the line of David. In Chronicles, which was written after Israel's return from exile, the focus is no longer David and his descendants but God himself. (When Nathan refers to *my* house, he does not mean his own! He is speaking for God, as all prophets did.)

It has been common practice among evangelicals to harmonize accounts such as these, for example, to say that somehow Nathan said both to David (perhaps he had two separate audiences with him) and that Samuel–Kings is reporting one speech while Chronicles is reporting the other. But such an explanation will run into many problems if it is applied consistently wherever one sees diverse accounts of the same phenomenon. To insist that, somehow, Samuel–Kings and Chronicles must say the same thing about the same event tells us more about the modern interpreter than it does about the biblical texts. Moreover, it flies in the face of both the evidence and common sense. The plain fact of the matter is that in Scripture we have two divergent accounts of the same event. The only question before us is how to handle this fact with integrity.

It may help to look at a more familiar example of this problem: the four Gospels. The fact is that there are four, not one, and they differ. For example, we have the well-known incident of Jesus cleansing the temple. In John it occurs at the beginning of Jesus' public ministry (John 2). In the other three Gospels it occurs at the end of Jesus' public ministry (the beginning of Passion Week). It is a distortion of the highest order to argue that Jesus must have cleansed the temple twice. For one thing, *none* of the Gospels say he did it twice. Second, although such a maneuver is motivated by the worthy desire to maintain the historical integrity of the Gospel accounts, it is based on an assumption about what constitutes good historiography that the Gospels themselves do not support, namely, that historiography must maintain chronological order.

A moment's examination will show that this is an unwarranted assumption. For example, when I come home from work, my wife may well ask how my day went. Here is one answer to that question:

Well, you'll never believe the traffic coming home. Horrible. But that was nothing compared to the drive in—so much construction. But the afternoon faculty meeting went well, and I was even able to finish my grading before it began. I also had lunch with some students and that was a good time.

Notice how I reported the "history" of my day to my wife. The first thing I reported was the last thing I did before I came home. Then I jumped to the morning commute, then to the afternoon faculty meeting, then to morning grading, then to lunch. Have I reported my day "inaccurately"? Am I "in error" because I did not maintain a rigid chronological sequence? Perhaps I reported my day in such a way to highlight what I felt was most important (I hate traffic jams with a fiery passion). Now imagine if my wife had called my departmental secretary to ask how my day went (not that the secretary can ever find me). She would get a very different reporting of the basic facts of my day, focusing no doubt on what I did while I was on campus, but it wouldn't be any less wrong.

Of course, the Bible is different. It is God's word. But what is true of all historiography is also true of biblical historiography—it is not objective. In fact—and this is getting more to the heart of the matter—in the strict sense of the word, there really is no such thing as objective historiography. Rather, all attempts to communicate the significance of historical events are shaped according to the historian's purpose. And in the Old Testament we see this not only in Samuel–Kings alone (as we saw above) but—as if the Holy Spirit could make it any more obvious—in the Bible's having different perspectives on the same historical events.

What makes biblical historiography the word of God is not that it is somehow immune from such things. It is God's word because it is—and this is how God did it. To be able to *confess* that the Bible is God's word is the gift of faith. To *understand* this confession is an ongoing process of greater clarification and insight, a process that will not end. Whether biblical historiography conforms to our expectations of how it should look is not the point. The point is that our expectations should be informed by how the Bible in fact behaves and by seeing that behavior, as best we can, in the historical context in which the Bible was written.

Predictably, this raises the very good issue of the relationship between the text of the Bible and the events it reports. So, what did Nathan *actually* say? What 2 Samuel reports? What 1 Chronicles reports? Neither? A little of both? The answer is, "I don't know, and neither does anyone else." In fact, I am beginning to suspect that this is not the primary question the Bible is set up to answer. I am by no means saying that history does not matter. I am saying that the *reporting* of historical events—historiography—always involves the shaping of history for particular purposes. How much shaping goes on in the Bible and for what purpose is no doubt the topic of ongoing discussion. In the case of Samuel–Kings and Chronicles, I gave the explanation of their differing purposes that I feel makes the best sense of the evidence. But *how* we answer that question, as such answers may shift over time, is not nearly as important as the posture from which we attempt these answers: that we fully respect the Bible as God's word at the outset, not *because* we can make sense of it all but *despite* our inability to do so at times.

How Does This Affect Us?

What can we take away from all this? There are three points I would like to focus on in conclusion.

First, a contemporary evangelical doctrine of Scripture must account for the Old Testament as an ancient Near Eastern phenomenon by going beyond the mere *observation* of that fact to allowing that fact to affect how we think about Scripture. A doctrine of Scripture that does not think through this incarnational dimension is inadequate in light of the evidence we have.

Second, such a worked-out doctrine of Scripture should have implications for how Christians today use it. In other words, understanding the Old Testament in its ancient Near Eastern setting will raise the question of how normative certain portions of the Old Testament are: if the Old Testament is a cultural phenomenon, how binding is it upon us whose cultural landscape is quite different?

This is a large issue, and I hesitate to bring it up because a full treatment would take us much further afield than we wish to go. (Also, we'll have a chance to look at this issue from different angles in chapters 3 and 4.) But the bottom line is this: how we conceive of the normativity or authority of the Old Testament must be in continual conversation with the incarnate dimension of Scripture. In other words, what the Bible *is* should affect what we as Christians *do* with it. It simply will not do to assume that what was binding on Israel is binding on us because it is written in the Bible, and the Bible is God's word, and therefore all of it is of equal weight through all time. Not only do we no longer share the conventions of the ancient Near Eastern world, but we also live in union with the crucified and risen Christ, in whom all of the Old Testament finds its completion (see chapter 4).

All this is to say that the central function of the Old Testament may not be there to "tell us what to do." It may be more a part of a larger story that God brings to an end many hundreds of years later in Christ. And this story, which ends with the incarnation of God's Son, had an incarnational dimension from the start.

Third, the incarnational dimension of Scripture continues today. Of course, the canon is closed—I am not disputing that for one moment. But, if *even the Bible* is a cultural phenomenon through and through, we should not be surprised to see that our own theological thinking is wrapped in cultural clothing as well. This is why every generation of Christians in every cultural context must seek to see how God is speaking to them in and through Scripture. It is not that the Bible is a timeless, contextless how-to book that we are meant to apply to today's world. Rather, the Bible itself demonstrates the inevitable cultural dimension of any expression of the gospel. This is not to say that the meaning of the gospel shifts with every cultural wind. It simply means that each generation, by the power of God's Spirit, has to make the gospel message its own by wrestling with how the gospel connects with the world in which that generation is living.

Further Reading

Biran, Avraham, and Joseph Naveh. "An Aramaic Stele Fragment from Tel Dan." *Israel Exploration Journal* 43 (1993): 81–98.

> The initial scholarly report on the Tel Dan Inscription.

Childs, Brevard S. *Myth and Reality in the Old Testament*. Studies in Biblical Theology 27. London: SCM, 1960.

> Although there will always be points of disagreement, Childs's treatment of myth and the Old Testament may still be the best little book (about one hundred pages) on the subject. The last four pages, entitled "The Theological Implications of Our Approach to Reality," speak of Christ as "the new reality."

Dearman, Andrew, ed. *Studies in the Mesha Inscription and Moab*. Atlanta: Scholars Press, 1989.

> A good place to start to understand the Mesha Inscription and the history surrounding it.

Dillard, Raymond B. "The Chronicler's Solomon." *Westminster Theological Journal* 43 (1980): 289–300.

> An excellent introduction to how Chronicles handles Israel's history, using the reign of Solomon as an example.

Fleming, Dan. "Genesis in History." *Westminster Theological Journal* 65 (2003): 251–62.

> Fleming is an expert on the ancient culture of Mari, another ancient culture, near Nuzi, that flourished in the eighteenth century BC. Here he looks at how the evidence from Mari affects our understanding of the nature of history in the Genesis account of Israel's first ancestors. He argues that the Mari evidence helps establish historical roots to Israel's ancestors, even though the written form of the accounts in Genesis reflects the first-millennium date of composition.

Gunkel, Hermann. *The Legends of Genesis*. Translated by W. H. Carruth. Chicago: Open Court, 1901.

> Gunkel was a highly influential German Old Testament scholar. This book (a translation of the introduction to his commentary on Genesis) is a landmark study. It is readable in style but challenging in its concepts.

Heidel, Alexander. *The Babylonian Genesis: The Story of Creation*. 2nd ed. Chicago: University of Chicago Press, 1951.

————. *The Gilgamesh Epic and Old Testament Parallels*. Chicago: University of Chicago Press, 1949.

> Heidel was an expert in ancient Mesopotamian literature. His view is that the dependence of the Old Testament on ancient Near Eastern texts cannot be demonstrated. Still, they all share similar concepts.

Hess, Richard W., and D. T. Tsumura, eds. *"I Studied Inscriptions from before the Flood": Ancient Near Eastern, Literary, and Linguistic Approaches to Genesis 1–11*. Winona Lake, IN: Eisenbrauns, 1994.

> Excellent resource for understanding contemporary study of Genesis 1–11. The opening essay by Hess ("One Hundred Fifty Years of Comparative Studies on Genesis 1–11: An Overview") is a succinct introduction to the history of scholarship.

King, Philip J., and Lawrence E. Stager. *Life in Biblical Israel*. Louisville: Westminster John Knox, 2001.

> An engaging look at the everyday life of ancient Israelites, complete with many photographs and drawings. Its focus is on the Iron Age, the period between 1200 BC and 586 BC (from the period of the judges to Israel's exile to Babylon).

Kline, Meredith G. *Treaty of the Great King*. Grand Rapids: Eerdmans, 1963.

> A good source for the relationship between Deuteronomy/Ten Commandments and the Hittite treaties.

Long, V. Philips. *The Art of Biblical History*. Foundations of Contemporary Interpretation 5. Grand Rapids: Zondervan, 1994.

> A great place to begin to explore what it meant in the ancient world to write history. Long's examples focus on the monarchy.

Middleton, J. Richard. *The Liberating Image: The* Imago Dei *in Genesis 1*. Grand Rapids: Brazos, 2005.

> Middleton looks at the idea of the "image of God" in Genesis 1–11 in the context of ancient Near Eastern religions. He concludes that Israel's theological traditions are articulated in conscious opposition to the ideological categories of Mesopotamia. In contrast to Mesopotamian ideology, Israel's story promotes the dignity of all humans, not just that of the royal or priestly classes. Middleton also outlines some ethical implications for today.

Morrison, Martha A. "Nuzi." Volume 4 / pages 1156–62 in *The Anchor Bible Dictionary*. Edited by David Noel Freedman et al. New York: Doubleday, 1992.

> Good introduction to the relevance of the Nuzi material to the Genesis account of Israel's early ancestors.

Murphy, Roland E. *The Tree of Life: An Exploration of Biblical Wisdom Literature*. 2nd ed. Grand Rapids: Eerdmans, 1996.

> On pages 23–24, Murphy looks at the parallels between Proverbs and *Amenemope*. His source is G. Bryce, *A Legacy of Wisdom* (Lewisburg: Bucknell, 1979), 101–11.

Walton, John H. *Ancient Israelite Literature in Its Cultural Context: A Survey of Parallels between Biblical and Ancient Near Eastern Texts*. Grand Rapids: Zondervan, 1989.

> An excellent and accessible compilation of ancient Near Eastern texts that parallel the Old Testament. The chapters are divided according to genre (e.g., cosmology, law, wisdom). The relevant ancient Near Eastern texts are listed, including such information as the date of composition and general content. Walton also offers his opinions concerning the degree to which the ancient Near Eastern and Old Testament texts are dependent on one another.

Young, Davis A. *The Biblical Flood: A Case Study of the Church's Response to Extrabiblical Evidence*. Grand Rapids: Eerdmans, 1995.

> Young is a professor of geology at Calvin College. This book is an honest and sophisticated attempt to bring the biblical flood story into conversation with the geological evidence and to encourage Christians not to think of the biblical story in isolation from the evidence.

The last four books listed are some of the more important sources for the ancient texts discussed in this chapter. Pritchard is the older, standard work. Hallo and Younger is a recent scholarly translation. Arnold and Beyer compile translations from various sources into a handy (and affordable) volume.

Arnold, Bill T., and Bryan E. Beyer, eds. *Readings from the Ancient Near East*. Grand Rapids: Baker, 2002.

Hallo, William W., and K. L. Younger Jr., eds. *The Context of Scripture*. 3 vols. Leiden: Brill, 1997–2002.

Pritchard, James, ed. *Ancient Near Eastern Texts Relating to the Old Testament*. 3rd ed. Princeton: Princeton University Press, 1969.

———. *The Ancient Near East in Pictures Relating to the Old Testament*. 2nd ed. Princeton: Princeton University Press, 1969.

3

The Old Testament and Theological Diversity

The Problem of Theological Diversity in the Old Testament

While I was in graduate school, one of my professors (a traditional Jewish scholar) said something that has stuck with me. This may sound terribly self-absorbed, but it was one of those "aha" moments that generated a process of rethinking a few things:

> For Jews, the Bible is a problem to be solved. For Christians, it is a message to be proclaimed.

This professor was referring to the history of Jewish biblical interpretation. It began centuries before Christ, and we see evidence of Jewish interpretive activity in such collections of writings as the **Apocrypha**, **Pseudepigrapha**, and Dead Sea Scrolls. In fact, within the Old Testament itself we see later authors interpreting earlier ones, a phenomenon usually referred to as "**innerbiblical interpretation**."

Those familiar with this history know that much Jewish interpretation is concerned to address problems of biblical interpretation. These problems arise, for example, because of the inherent ambiguities in the Hebrew language—something every Hebrew student is well aware of. (Knowing the original Hebrew does not always make the text "come alive"! It often introduces obscurities that English readers are not aware of.) Other difficulties arise from points of tension that exist between parts of the Old Testament itself.

A look at the major Jewish texts that engage in biblical interpretation (**Mishnah**, **Talmud**, **midrashic** literature) reveals an approach to biblical interpretation that, among other things, expends tremendous energy in engaging these tensions and ambiguities. In fact, these ancient interpreters seem to revel in the chance to do so; the Bible itself, precisely because of its inherent ambiguities and tensions, is believed to *invite* problem solving. And if one were to look closely at some of these Jewish interpretive texts, one would see that these biblical tensions and ambiguities are solved in multiple—even contradictory—ways, and these solutions are allowed to remain side by side in these authoritative canons of Jewish tradition. The stress seems to be *not* on solving the problems once and for all but on a community upholding a *conversation* with Scripture with creative energy.

Although I am not holding up this Jewish model of handling interpretive difficulties as an ultimate standard, I have learned much from studying this history. Of course, there is much more to it than what I describe here. One other very important matter will be addressed in chapter 4: the relation of Jewish interpretation to early Christian interpretation of the Old Testament. At this juncture I simply wish to make the observation that Christianity, at least the Christianity with which modern evangelicalism is familiar, followed a different path. As quite distinct from Jewish interpretation, the history of modern evangelical interpretation exhibits a strong degree of discomfort with the tensions and ambiguities of Scripture. The assumptions often made are that Scripture should have no tensions and that any such tensions are not real but introduced from the outside, namely, by scholarship hostile to evangelical Christianity. Whatever tensions remain are addressed either by posing some direct solution (however ingenious) or by moving the problem to the side ("We know it has to fit somehow; we just aren't sure how").

Our history of interpretation, therefore, is not a catalog of diverse engagements of tensions and ambiguities in the Old Testament. The Christian task has been more defined by relegating such tensions and ambiguities to the background in favor of proclaiming a unified message. After all, the Old Testament is not there to set us on an interpretive adventure, but to tell us what God is like, what he has done, who we are as his people, and what we are to do in response. What is needed is *unity*, a message. If the Bible is written ultimately by one author, God, there is little room for tensions.

In a word, the contrast between Judaism and Christianity is in how they handle the *diversity* of Scripture, by which I mean the Old Testament's different perspectives or points of view on the same topic. A similar distinction can be made between critical scholarship and evangelicalism. One way that critical biblical scholarship takes diversity into account is to say that the Old Testament is full of contradictions and, hence, a quaint record of conflicting human opinions. Such an approach will never be an acceptable option for Christian thinking. An evangelical counterattack, however, is to defend the Bible against accusations of diversity by showing that such diversity is not there, involves only minor issues, or can be resolved in theory at some future time. But this alternative creates tensions of its own, and it runs the risk of avoiding the difficult issues altogether.

It is a great irony that both the critical and evangelical options (as distinct from the Jewish model) take part in the same assumption: God's word and diversity at the level of factual content and theological message are incompatible. I reject this assumption for the simple reason that I see no good reason to hold it, particularly since—as I hope to show below—diversity is such a well-documented phenomenon in the Old Testament. It seems to me that a false assumption of how the Bible *ought* to behave stands behind this critical and evangelical view. As a corrective, one must observe how Scripture *does* behave and draw conclusions from that.

My aim in this chapter is to outline some examples of diversity in the Old Testament in order to demonstrate that diversity is inherent to the text and not imposed onto the Bible from outside attacks on its unity. Further, any evangelical view of Scripture must take this diversity into account, since it is an important part of Scripture's own dynamic. It is not simply a question of acknowledging diversity and then setting it aside at a safe distance. Rather, it is to ask what such diversity tells us about what the Bible is and who God is—a God who has given us Scripture that looks like this.

The examples I have chosen are not necessarily the most interesting for everyone, nor do I necessarily think they are the most challenging. I have chosen them because I think they provide a clear entryway into this topic. Further, in the pages that follow, you will not find *final* answers to these types of questions. An incarnational approach to Scripture is not a magic key of some sort to wipe away troubles quickly and easily. But as we look at examples of diversity, taken from various sections of the Old Testament, I will make suggestions along the way as to how an incarnational approach can foster a better theological environment for handling diversity. I hope this will be helpful for readers seeking to work through important issues of Old Testament interpretation for themselves.

Diversity in Wisdom Literature

I would like to begin by looking at a portion of the Old Testament where diversity is fairly widely recognized: wisdom literature (Proverbs, Ecclesiastes, and Job). By exploring this diversity first, perhaps we will be able to look at more problematic examples elsewhere in the Old Testament in a slightly different light.

Proverbs

Proverbs is a book that can easily be misunderstood as a how-to book or "rules to live by." There is no question that Proverbs is very much concerned to communicate matters of wise living, but there is more involved than simply "do what Proverbs says." For example, look at the contrast between Proverbs 26:4 and 26:5:

> Do not answer a fool according to his folly,
>   or you will be like him yourself.
>
> Answer a fool according to his folly,
>   or he will be wise in his own eyes.

Already we get a glimpse of the complexity involved in handling Proverbs. *Both* of these sayings are wise, even though—to state the obvious—they say the opposite. This one example already alerts readers that there is diversity within Proverbs. It is not just a book that hands out pearls of wisdom to be applied without further ado. Rather, the reader is expected to invest energy in *discerning whether a certain proverb is relevant for a certain situation*. To put it another way, there is more to wisdom than simply reading a *proverb*. One must also have the wisdom to read the *situation*, to know whether a proverb is fitting.

The wisdom in Proverbs reflects the diversity of situations we find ourselves in every day. For example, what movies one parent might allow his or her twelve-year-old to watch may differ from what other parents do with their children. When my son was twelve, he asked if we could watch *Saving Private Ryan* together. We did watch it, but before doing so I had to consider many factors. What is his personality type? What kind of internal "filters" does he have? Is this the right time and place to put him in a controlled setting to help him grow? In this case, watching that movie was a tremendously positive experience for him. (The opening battle scene was the most graphic representation of war he had ever seen, and it helped him understand something of how horrible war is.) Some might think that the violence and dialogue in the movie are inappropriate for a twelve-year-old. I certainly understand the point, but quoting Proverbs 22:6, as one shocked parent did, is not going to resolve the issue:

> Train a child in the way he should go,
>   and when he is old he will not turn from it.

Simply quoting this proverb will not do. It takes wisdom to know *how* this proverb applies to *this* situation, which means an intimate knowledge of the circumstances. In my opinion, I *did* apply the wisdom of Proverbs 22:6 by allowing my son to watch an R-rated movie.

Such diversity as we find in 26:4 and 26:5 is not hidden in a few corners of Proverbs, but is quite prevalent. Another example is what Proverbs says about wealth:

> The wealth of the rich is their fortified city,
>   but poverty is the ruin of the poor. (10:15)

> The wealth of the rich is their fortified city;
>   they imagine it an unscalable wall. (18:11)

The first proverb contrasts wealth and poverty. That wealth is the "fortified city" of the rich is seen as a positive thing, and this is contrasted with poverty, which ruins the poor in 10:15. In 18:11, however, the matter is quite the opposite. Whereas the first half of 18:11 restates the first half of 10:15 (both phrases are exactly the same in Hebrew), the second half of 18:11 draws a very different conclusion: the rich are chided for thinking their wealth is a "fortified city." The implication is that, for *some*, wealth is a source of security, a fortification from poverty (10:15). For *others*, however, their wealth is a source of arrogance: they feel that nothing can touch them in their fortress of riches (18:11).

Another kind of distinction about wealth is found in 10:16 and 11:4:

> The wages of the righteous bring them life,
>   but the income of the wicked brings them punishment. (10:16)

> Wealth is worthless in the day of wrath,
>   but righteousness delivers from death. (11:4)

In 10:16, we read that wealth is more or less neutral and that its benefits depend on the quality of the person possessing it, whether righteous or wicked. (In Proverbs, as well as in much of the Old Testament, "righteous" simply means to behave "rightly," whereas "wicked" means to behave unjustly.) Then in 11:4, we learn that any benefits that wealth might have are neutralized "in the day of wrath." It is not wealth per se that brings life or punishment, as 10:16 says; only righteousness can be counted on to deliver from death.

Then we have 11:28:

> Whoever trusts in his riches will fall,
> but the righteous will thrive like a green leaf.

Here we see that one's downfall is in trusting riches. The righteous, however, will thrive. There is no mention of whether the righteous have wealth. Apparently, somewhat similar to if not more explicit than 10:16, wealth is neutral and what counts is one's character. But then again, 19:4 seems to give an unqualified endorsement of the benefits of wealth, regardless of other factors:

> Wealth brings many friends,
> but a poor man's friend deserts him.

The point to be stressed here is that *all* of these proverbs are wise. *All* are correct. The question is not *whether* they are correct, but *when*. It is, therefore, wrong to think of "the teaching of Proverbs on wealth" with the expectation that all its statements about wealth "say the same thing" or are compatible on the level of isolated concepts. The wisdom derived from Proverbs on the question of wealth differs depending on what proverb you read. To isolate any one proverb and claim universal validity is in fact a fundamental misreading of the trajectory of the book. In other words, one cannot take 18:11, for example, and use it as a blanket condemnation of all who have wealth, nor can one isolate 10:15 to let a wealthy person off the hook who is arrogant, unjust, or otherwise unwise in his or her financial dealings.

It is not enough that these proverbs are "in the Bible" and therefore to be "applied in our lives." They are diverse sayings that require wisdom to know *how* to handle them correctly. To collate the diversity of Proverbs so that it yields a unified teaching on wealth is to render unimportant the diversity that God himself has put there. To miss the diversity is to miss the book of Proverbs.

Ecclesiastes

With Proverbs in mind it is helpful to move immediately to Ecclesiastes, since the two are often compared with one another. Ecclesiastes exhibits diversity on two levels: (1) diversity within the book itself and (2) diversity between the teachings of this book and mainstream Old Testament theology.

Concerning the first level, the tensions surrounding Ecclesiastes are nothing new to readers of the Bible. As far back as the early medieval period, Jewish commentators attempted to grapple with both internal inconsistencies and the relationship between Ecclesiastes and the rest of the Old Testament. An example cited in the Talmud is Ecclesiastes 7:3 and 8:15:

> Sorrow is better than laughter,
> because a sad face is good for the heart. (7:3)

> So I commend the enjoyment of life, because nothing is better for a man under the sun than to eat and drink and be glad. Then joy will accompany him in his work all the days of the life God has given him under the sun. (8:15)

An example of the tensions between Ecclesiastes and other portions of the Old Testament is Ecclesiastes 2:10, where **Qoheleth** (the main character of the book) claims to be investigating pleasure in order to find meaning, and he does so, as he claims, being guided by wisdom:

> I denied myself nothing my eyes desired;
> I refused my heart no pleasure.

On the surface at least this seems to be quite at odds with Numbers 15:39:

> You will have these tassels to look at and so you will remember all the commands of the LORD, that you may obey them and not prostitute yourselves by going after the lusts of your own hearts and eyes.

Regardless of how we might address these specific issues, the very fact that the history of Jewish and Christian interpretation felt the need to address them highlights the problem.

With respect to the internal tensions, many recent commentators (e.g., Michael Fox's *A Time to Tear Down and a Time to Build Up*) argue that the contradictions in Ecclesiastes are there for a reason. They are not there to be resolved. Rather, that there are contradictions in life is precisely what the author of Ecclesiastes intends his readers to see. When we look at Ecclesiastes from that perspective, we can see that our attempts to work out the contradictions fly in the face of what the book is doing. Qoheleth's observations—that life is unpredictable, uncontrollable, and contradictory—are the engine that drives the theology of the book. This is similar to what we saw with Proverbs: to invest energy in smoothing out the diversity of Proverbs or Ecclesiastes amounts to not reading these books but actually reading past them.

Both Ecclesiastes and Proverbs are wisdom books, so how do they square with one another? It is not the case, as some argue, that Proverbs provides a standard, unified presentation of wisdom and that Qoheleth distances himself from that portrayal. On one level, one can see how one *could* arrive at that conclusion from reading these passages in Ecclesiastes:

> For with much wisdom comes much sorrow;
>   the more knowledge, the more grief. (1:18)

> Do not be overrighteous,
>   neither be overwise—
>   why destroy yourself? (7:16)

One will not find such sentiments in Proverbs. But the matter is really much more complicated than this. For one thing, as we have seen regarding wealth, Proverbs is not a "flat" collection of sayings: diversity is already built into Proverbs. Second, it is not the case that Qoheleth attacks the kind of wisdom represented in Proverbs and makes that wisdom to be of no value. In fact, Qoheleth appeals to wisdom as he makes his investigation of life "under the sun" (1:13; 2:13). Both Ecclesiastes and Proverbs acknowledge the ups and downs of life, the complexity of living a good life in a harsh world.

This being said, however, Ecclesiastes is still different from Proverbs in at least one important, and fundamental, way. Proverbs hammers home again and again that "wisdom works," that it is always there and does not fail:

> Wisdom is supreme; therefore get wisdom.
>   Though it cost all you have, get understanding. (Prov. 4:7)

Such a view is what drives Proverbs, and it is a very different kind of opinion from what is expressed in Ecclesiastes 1:18 and 7:16. Qoheleth is not so sure that wisdom always works. In fact, he seems to resign himself to the notion that wisdom, although good *to a point*, ultimately won't bring home the goods. Why? Because Qoheleth observes that the wise life is not *always* rewarded as it should be. The just and wise person sometimes suffers while the unjust and unwise person sometimes succeeds. Wisdom does not *guarantee* a payoff, and this frustrates Qoheleth.

And if that weren't enough, Qoheleth observes that everyone—the wise and unwise—will die anyway. So, in the end, there really is no payoff for anything we do. (For what it's worth, Qoheleth clearly has no notion of the afterlife such as Christians take for granted—see 3:18–21.) This is the stark reality that is ultimately at the root of Qoheleth's recurring statement "meaningless, utterly meaningless" (New International Version; or "vanity of vanities" in the King James Version). Wisdom has benefits (2:13), but since the same fate (death) overtakes the foolish and the wise (2:14), there is *ultimately* nothing to be gained by being wise (2:15). Qoheleth resigns himself to the conclusion that wisdom, although *relatively* superior to foolishness, is not *ultimately* superior. Qoheleth does not gloat in that fact. Rather, he laments that this is the case.

So there are certainly differences between Ecclesiastes and Proverbs, but the point here is not to iron them out. What is important for us to keep in mind is that *both*, with their diverse points of view, are considered worthy to stand side by side in the Old Testament (at least in the English canonical order—the Jewish canonical order has Ruth and Song of Songs in between, but the point remains). *Both* Ecclesiastes and Proverbs are wise books. Qoheleth, despite his misgivings and apparent lapses into what seems to border on heresy, is called "wise" in 12:9–10:

> Not only was the Teacher [Hebrew *Qoheleth*] wise, but also he imparted knowledge to the people. He pondered and searched out and set in order many proverbs. The Teacher searched to find just the right words, and what he wrote was upright and true.

It will not do to dismiss Qoheleth as a fool himself, someone whose lack of faith will not allow him to see past the end of his nose. He is rather a wise man who observes true inconsistencies in life. The end of the book does not cancel out the words of Qoheleth, as is sometimes thought. Instead, the words of Qoheleth are put into a broader perspective. Despite the inconsistencies of life that really are there—and pointing them out is a wisdom task (as Qoheleth has done)—at the end of the day, the book of Ecclesiastes calls upon all to work through the struggles by remaining fearful of God and obedient to him:

> Now all has been heard;
> here is the conclusion of the matter:

> Fear God and keep his commandments,
>   for this is the whole duty of man.
> For God will bring every deed into judgment,
>   including every hidden thing,
>   whether it is good or evil. (12:13–14)

With Proverbs and Ecclesiastes as partners in the same canon, diversity should not be thought of as a problem to be explained away, but welcomed as an indication of the character of God's word. Diversity is woven into Old Testament literature. But note that diversity in no way implies chaos or error. This whole discussion is to help move us away from such an assumption. We should resist the temptation of thinking of the word of God as being necessarily free from diversity in content because God would not or could not inspire such a thing. Such thinking would clearly pose problems such as those we read in Ecclesiastes.

The book's internal tensions as well as external tensions with Proverbs and other Old Testament theologies surely must be more than simply a sorry state of affairs that we have to endure. Rather, to respect the diversity of the Old Testament is to respect it the way God has given it to us. And if we employ the incarnational analogy, we can see that the Bible reflects diversity because the human drama in which God participates is likewise diverse. I have found it helpful to keep this in mind as I read portions of the Old Testament that do not seem to square well with others.

Job

The final wisdom text we will look at is the book of Job, and this book is an example of diversity of another sort. Much of the Old Testament presents the notion that deeds have consequences. A good place to see this is Deuteronomy 5:32–33:

> So be careful to do what the LORD your God has commanded you; do not turn aside to the right or to the left. Walk in all the way that the LORD your God has commanded you, so that you may live and prosper and prolong your days in the land that you will possess.

Israel's very existence was tied to the consequences of following God's law. In fact, the possession of the land hung in the balance (Deut. 28:64–68). Israel would be punished for disobedience and blessed for obedience. This is very much in harmony with what we find in Proverbs:

> My son, do not forget my teaching,
>> but keep my commands in your heart,
> for they will prolong your life many years
>> and bring you prosperity. (Prov. 3:1–2)

Keeping the father's wise commands results in long life and prosperity.

The book of Job seems to present a different picture of the relationship between deeds and their consequences. Job's friends (Eliphaz, Bildad, Zophar, and Elihu), unaware as they are of the ultimate cause of Job's suffering (God allows "the accuser" to afflict Job; see Job 1–2), observe Job's suffering and conclude that he must have done something to deserve it. And, when we keep in view what we read in places like Deuteronomy 5:32–33 and Proverbs 3:1–2, we can certainly understand why they would arrive at such a conclusion. If disobedience leads to God's curse (Deut. 28:15–68), then it is not too hard to reason back the other way: if you are cursed, you must have done something to deserve it.

This is the assumption that fuels the dialogues between Job and his friends in Job 3–37. Because we, the readers of Job, know the cause of Job's suffering from reading Job 1–2, we may be tempted to dismiss too quickly the arguments of his friends as off the mark. But we must remember that all they saw was the result. Anyone well versed in Old Testament teaching would likely have drawn the same conclusion. Here is some of what Job's friends have to say:

> Blessed is the man whom God corrects;
>> so do not despise the discipline of the Almighty.
> For he wounds, but he also binds up;
>> he injures, but his hands also heal. (Eliphaz in Job 5:17–18)

> Surely God does not reject a blameless man
>> or strengthen the hands of evildoers.
> He will yet fill your mouth with laughter
>> and your lips with shouts of joy.
> Your enemies will be clothed in shame,
>> and the tents of the wicked will be no more. (Bildad in Job 8:20–22)

> Yet if you devote your heart to him
>> and stretch out your hands to him,
> if you put away the sin that is in your hand
>> and allow no evil to dwell in your tent,
> then you will lift up your face without shame;
>> you will stand firm and without fear. (Zophar in Job 11:13–15)

> God is mighty, but does not despise men;
>> he is mighty, and firm in his purpose.

He does not keep the wicked alive
　but gives the afflicted their rights.
He does not take his eyes off the righteous;
　he enthrones them with kings
　and exalts them forever. (Elihu in Job 36:5–7)

What is wrong with their advice? In the *abstract*, nothing, but that is precisely the point. Job's friends express what seems utterly true; one would not blink if one were reading Deuteronomy and came across such statements. In a way, they are well within their biblical right to draw the conclusion they do. But Job's suffering is not in the abstract. As readers of the book of Job know, as well as Job himself, whatever the reasons for his suffering, it is not because he has been disobedient.

Job's friends were not wrong in thinking that God blesses obedience and punishes disobedience. They were wrong in appealing to this principle *superficially*, without sufficient knowledge of the *particulars of the situation*. There is a deed-consequence pattern in the Old Testament, as we see in Deuteronomy and Proverbs, but it cannot be applied *rigidly*. There is much more to the book of Job than this, but it seems that one point it makes is to warn against a superficial application of this pattern in any and every situation. It is not that the book of Job disagrees with, say, Deuteronomy or Proverbs. Rather, it is reminding us that there is another side to the matter: it takes wisdom to know how and when the deed-consequence pattern is to be discerned. In this sense, the diversity of Job is not that it counters Deuteronomy, but that it adds a real-life dimension to the question of human activity and its consequences. If it were not for books like Job, we might fall into the trap that Job's friends fell into, thinking that the Bible—and by implication God himself—is one dimensional, disconnected from the complexities of human existence. But I suggest here again that the Bible is diverse because life is. And God does not shy away from it.

Having begun our discussion of diversity by looking at wisdom literature, we can now move beyond wisdom literature to some other examples.

Diversity in Chronicles

In the last chapter we looked at Chronicles to see what we can learn about historiography. Now we can briefly revisit Chronicles in the context of theological diversity of the Old Testament. As we have seen, what makes Chronicles so challenging is that it presents an alternate history of Israel from that found in Samuel–Kings. As stated before, the writer of Chronicles has a different immediate audience to speak to: postexilic Israelites. Therefore the book presents a different interpretation of events leading up to Israel's exile that gives hope and covenantal meaning to those returning to the land.

It is widely recognized that Samuel and Kings, as well as Joshua and Judges, are united by many theological themes. In fact, these books exhibit enough theological and stylistic similarities that many scholars consider them to be the work of one person (or a group of people working together). This version of Israel's history is normally referred to as the "**Deuteronomistic History**" because this piece of historiography seems to reflect some key emphases of the book of Deuteronomy.

One important emphasis that Samuel–Kings specifically shares with Deuteronomy is that Israel must worship in a *central* location (presumably, the temple in Jerusalem, although it is not mentioned by name). The tabernacle was a transportable structure and thus appropriate for a desert-wandering people. But now that the Israelites are settled in the land, in its place is a permanent structure, the temple. Deuteronomy 12 makes it clear that, after entering the land, Israel's worship is to be centralized in the temple in Jerusalem (or as Deut. 12:5 puts it: "The place the LORD your God will choose from among all your tribes to put his Name there for his dwelling"). A good example of this emphasis can be seen in the Passover law. In Exodus 12, when the Israelites were leaving Egypt and about to embark on a desert journey, the meal was to be celebrated in the *family* (Exod. 12:2–4). On the other hand, Deuteronomy 16, where the possession of the promised land was already in view, is very emphatic that the Passover be celebrated not "in any town" but "in the place he will choose as a dwelling for his Name," that is, the Jerusalem temple (Deut. 16:5–6).

One of the bases by which the kings in Samuel–Kings were evaluated was how faithful they were in centralizing Israel's worship. They were to destroy the high places where the Canaanite gods were worshiped (by means of sacrifices) and worship only in Jerusalem. Of the twenty [counting Tibni, 1 Kings 16:21–22] northern kings, only Hoshea and Shallum made an attempt to do so. Of the twenty southern kings, Hezekiah and Josiah did the best. Six others suppressed idolatry but did not remove the high places. The remaining twelve did nothing.

Again, as we saw in the previous chapter, the purpose of Samuel–Kings, at least in part, was to *explain the exile to an exilic audience*. Taking 2 Kings 25:27–30 at face value, Samuel–Kings ends in the middle of the exile, in the thirty-seventh year of the exile of Jehoiachin, the last king of Judah (around 560 BC). So, to the question "What happened to drive us out of the promised land?" the answer was that Israel and its leaders were not faithful to God's covenant. They continued worshiping false gods rather than the true God who brought them out of Egypt.

Chronicles is a different matter. Here Israel's history is written from the point of view of those who have *returned* to the land after being released from Babylon. The burning question was not, "What did we do to get us kicked out of the land?" but, "Now that we are back, what do we do?"; or, perhaps a better way of putting it, "Who are we? Are we still God's people? How can we be sure he'll have us back?" Some of Chronicles' differing emphases are as follows:

1. *Chronicles greatly diminishes the sins of David.* For example, the author of Chronicles does not mention the sin of David with Bathsheba. His focus is not on what contributed to bringing Israel to exile. Rather, David (and Solomon) are portrayed as glorified figures. They have become "messianic" figures, models of ideal kingship who embodied the hopes of the returnees.

2. *Chronicles emphasizes the unity of God's people.* For example, the transition of power from David to Solomon is smooth and receives enthusiastic support from *all* the people. There is nothing in Chronicles about the power struggles recorded in 1 Kings 1–2. Chronicles' emphasis on the unity of God's people is understandable in view of the postexilic setting of the book. Israel is now to be *one people*, not given to political factions. Now is the time to rebuild the kingdom, to relive an ideal age, not to disintegrate into petty, warring factions.

3. *Chronicles strongly emphasizes the temple and Solomon's role in building it.* Chronicles' purpose in emphasizing this role is to reestablish the central importance of proper worship and the king's role in bringing this about, which is precisely what the preexilic kings of Samuel–Kings did not do.

4. *Chronicles emphasizes a theology of "immediate retribution."* Much more so than Samuel–Kings, Chronicles preaches that you are punished for your own sins and, likewise, rewarded for obedience. One of the purposes of such an emphasis is to tell the postexilic community that obedience is vital to their national rebirth. Also, the sins of the preexilic Israelites are now wiped clean. The postexilic Israelites will not be held responsible for the sins of their ancestors. For example, 2 Chronicles 15:1–2, speaking of King Asa, records these words, which are not found in 1 Kings 15:13–16:

The Spirit of God came upon [the prophet] Azariah son of Oded. He went out to meet Asa and said to him, "Listen to me, Asa and all Judah and

Benjamin. The LORD is with you when you are with him. If you seek him, he will be found by you, but if you forsake him, he will forsake you."

Other things could be added to this list, in terms of both breadth and depth. The basic point, however, is that there is considerable theological diversity between the two accounts of Israel's history. They are both accounts of history, but they differ significantly because their purposes differ (to pick up on the discussion in chapter 2). However much we might struggle with this, it is important to understand that God himself is pleased to allow this tension to stand. To acknowledge this freely is the proper starting point for any further discussion.

Diversity in Law

One of the more interesting places in the Old Testament where we find diversity is in portions of the law. If there is any place in the Old Testament where we would *not* expect diversity, it is in the law. I have often heard the argument put something like this:

After all, the law is very different from wisdom literature or Chronicles. It is God's direct communication to the Israelites about what they should and shouldn't do; it reveals God's very will to his people; obedience brought blessing, disobedience brought curse. If there is any portion of God's word that demands consistency, it is the law. If the law is inconsistent, that would mean God is inconsistent. But since that cannot be, it must be that the law only appears to be inconsistent.

Perhaps. But many assumptions are being made in such an argument— for example, that diversity implies inconsistency, which naturally raises the issue of error. I would rather look at the issue differently: if *even* the law shows clear marks of diversity, what does this tell us about the nature of Scripture and the nature of the God who reveals himself there?

Let us look first at some commonly accepted examples of diversity in Israel's legal texts. This is certainly not exhaustive but merely representative, and any one point could certainly entertain further discussion.

The Ten Commandments

The giving of the Ten Commandments is recorded twice, in Exodus 20:2–17 and Deuteronomy 5:6–21. Although there are no differences in the order or basic content of the commandments, there are noticeable differences in the wording (in italic type) of the fourth, fifth, and tenth commandments:

Commandment	Exodus	Deuteronomy
4	*Remember* the Sabbath day by keeping it holy. Six days you shall labor and do all your work, but the seventh day is a Sabbath to the LORD your God. On it you shall not do any work, neither you, nor your son or daughter, nor your manservant or maidservant, nor your animals, nor the alien within your gates. *For in six days the LORD made the heavens and the earth, the sea, and all that is in them, but he rested on the seventh day.* Therefore the LORD blessed the Sabbath day and made it holy. (20:8–11)	*Observe* the Sabbath day by keeping it holy, *as the LORD your God has commanded you.* Six days you shall labor and do all your work, but the seventh day is a Sabbath to the LORD your God. On it you shall not do any work, neither you, nor your son or daughter, nor your manservant or maidservant, *nor your ox, your donkey* or any of your animals, nor the alien within your gates, *so that your manservant and maidservant may rest, as you do. Remember that you were slaves in Egypt and that the LORD your God brought you out of there with a mighty hand and an outstretched arm.* Therefore the LORD your God has commanded you to observe the Sabbath day. (5:12–15)
5	Honor your father and your mother, so that you may live long in the land the LORD your God is giving you. (20:12)	Honor your father and your mother, *as the LORD your God has commanded you*, so that you may live long *and that it may go well with you* in the land the LORD your God is giving you. (5:16)
10	You shall not covet your neighbor's house. You shall not covet your neighbor's wife, or his manservant or maidservant, his ox or donkey, or anything that belongs to your neighbor. (20:17)	You shall not covet your neighbor's wife. *You shall not set your desire on your neighbor's house or land*, his manservant or maidservant, his ox or donkey, or anything that belongs to your neighbor. (5:21)

On the one hand, these differences do not affect the content of the laws. For example, the differences in the fifth commandment are certainly inconsequential. And with the fourth commandment, is it really all that big of a difference between "Remember the Sabbath" and "Observe the Sabbath"? And is it all that important that Deuteronomy adds "as the LORD your God has commanded you" in commandments

4 and 5? Moreover, the preamble and commandments 1–3 and 6–9 are identical.

Exodus and Deuteronomy may be identical in general content and even in wording in most of the commandments. But one might well wonder why there are *any* differences between the wordings of the commandments. After all, isn't the wording important? Why would God's revelation of his Ten Commandments, the bedrock of his law, have *any* differences? Wouldn't this simply confuse people? And the differences between the two versions of the fourth commandment transcend any mere difference in wording: the motives differ. For Exodus, the motive for keeping the Sabbath is God's rest on the seventh day of creation. In Deuteronomy, the motive is to make sure that the Israelites' servants would rest just as the Israelites themselves do.

We must also take note of the way in which the Ten Commandments in Deuteronomy are introduced. We do not have here the direct revelation from God on Sinai, as is the case in Exodus, but *Moses recounting* that experience for the Israelites who are now forty years removed from that event. And, regardless of what theory of pentateuchal authorship one subscribes to, the simple fact of the matter is that *Deuteronomy presents Moses as someone who, forty years after the fact, recounts God's words differently than they were given in Exodus*. There is diversity even in the Ten Commandments.

One explanation for this difference is that the speech of Moses recorded in Deuteronomy expands Exodus by making more explicit Israel's obligation to make sure that all those who work—whether children, servants, or animals—get their proper rest of one day in seven. One can also appeal to the different settings of Exodus and Deuteronomy, the latter having in view the more immediate occupation of the land. Such an explanation is analogous to what we have seen with respect to the differing histories in Chronicles and Samuel–Kings: they look different because they are written for different purposes and at different times. But again, the problem with the Ten Commandments is that we are not talking about ancient Israelite historians writing to encourage their community, but the biblical claim that God himself is revealing his law to his people.

This brings us to the following observation: God seems to be perfectly willing to allow his law to be adjusted over time. Perhaps Israel, standing virtually on the brink of the promised land in Deuteronomy, needed to hear the fourth commandment a bit differently. For the previous forty years they had been a desert-dwelling people. But now they are about to take possession of a land. They will be the owners, and their menservants and maidservants will be working for them. So, at this juncture, what

Israel needs to hear loud and clear is: "Don't become comfortable and arrogant and oppress your servants as the Egyptians did to you."

In other words, there seems to be a situational dimension to law, just as we saw with wisdom literature. Law is God's revelation, but does that necessarily imply that it is static and unbending? Perhaps God himself understands—and in fact shows us—that even the law has a situational dimension. For any biblical law we can think of, obedience is much more than simply "Do what it says." One must also understand whether the present situation calls for that law and then *how* that law is to be kept. Few Christians would have any argument against the sixth commandment, but believing it in principle is very different from acting upon it. Is capital punishment murder? What about abortion? What about protecting your family against an intruder? What about war? When we put flesh on the bare bones of the Ten Commandments, we see that there is a "wisdom dimension" to any attempt to keep the law. To say this is not to dismiss the law but to recognize the inevitable, that keeping the law is not a mechanical, legalistic process.

Before we leave the Ten Commandments, we should look at one very concrete biblical example of how situations affect the keeping of the law. In both Exodus and Deuteronomy there is a consequence explicitly attached to the second commandment:

> For I, the LORD your God, am a jealous God, punishing the children for the sin of the fathers to the third and fourth generation of those who hate me, but showing love to a thousand generations of those who love me and keep my commandments. (Exod. 20:5–6/Deut. 5:9–10)

The point is fairly clear: the idolatry of one generation is punishable to the "third and fourth generation," but to those who keep the commandments, God will show love "to a thousand generations." There is some discussion whether "third and fourth generation" should be taken literally (especially since "a thousand generations" seems not to be literal), but that is beside the point here. What the second commandment says is that the actions of one generation, for good or ill, will affect how God deals with subsequent generations.

Compare this with Ezekiel 18, where Ezekiel relates to the people God's word to him that "the soul who sins is the one who will die" (18:4). He then describes three generations of Israelites: the first is righteous (by which he means obeys the law), the second violent, the third righteous again. The point Ezekiel makes, quite adamantly, is that the second (violent) generation does *not* benefit from the righteousness of the first, nor is the third (righteous) generation punished for the wickedness of the second:

Yet you ask, "Why does the son not share the guilt of his father?" Since the son has done what is just and right and has been careful to keep all my decrees, he will surely live. The soul who sins is the one who will die. The son will not share the guilt of the father, nor will the father share the guilt of the son. The righteousness of the righteous man will be credited to him, and the wickedness of the wicked will be charged against him. (Ezek. 18:19–20)

The stark contrast between Ezekiel and the second commandment even gave some early rabbis pause to question whether Ezekiel was authoritative. But there is more to this than simply whether Ezekiel contradicts the second commandment. I venture to guess that Ezekiel was quite aware of the second commandment. In fact, I suggest that he was consciously addressing it. His problem, however, is not with the second commandment itself but with those who appeal to it in a mechanical manner, perhaps in an attempt to excuse themselves from the consequences of their actions. Ezekiel's response, perhaps also to be read, along with Chronicles, in the context of national rebuilding, is, "Don't hide behind the law. You are still responsible for keeping it."

The reason why Exodus and Deuteronomy don't address the possible abuses of "generational consequences" as Ezekiel does is that such abuses would have been beside the point. How would it be if, after Exodus 20:6, we would have read, "Of course, such a promise as this is subject to abuse, so don't get too comfortable with this." The law is the law, and it is stated succinctly. But, as future generations work out what it means to keep that law—as situations and circumstances change—it is not enough simply to *read* the law. Rather, it must be *interpreted*. And any attempt to interpret the law is necessarily an interaction between the law itself and the circumstances to which it is being applied. Ezekiel's words are instructive to us precisely because they are so extreme. To address his own context, where the second commandment was being abused, the prophet speaks in a way that relativizes the letter of that commandment.

Even the Ten Commandments are open to diverse handling depending on the situation being addressed. To acknowledge such diversity is not to dismiss the law but to uphold it in a manner in which the Old Testament does. For Christians, there is an added dimension that must be addressed as well: how we now relate to the law in light of our union with the crucified and risen Christ. To address this issue in any depth in a brief book such as this would take us far afield. Still, it is worth pausing for a moment to note that the gospel, without diminishing the law, encourages further flexibility. For example, Jesus claims to be "Lord of the Sabbath" (Luke 6:5). Whatever problems he might have had with the Pharisees' interpretation of the Sabbath law (6:1–4), Jesus does not argue that they are handling the Sabbath law *incorrectly*. Rather he tells them that he, being the Son of Man (6:5), has authority *over* the Sabbath. This suggests that, with the coming of Christ, there is a higher authority to which Christians submit, the law of the risen Christ, in whom the law of God is perfectly fulfilled.

Slaves

In Exodus 21:2, we read:

> If you buy a Hebrew servant, he is to serve you for six years. But in the seventh year, he shall go free, without paying anything.

In Exodus 21:4, 7, we read that the female slave may not go free:

> Only the man shall go free. . . . If a man sells his daughter as a servant, she is not to go free as menservants do.

Compare this with Deuteronomy 15:12:

> If a fellow Hebrew, a man or a woman, sells himself to you and serves you six years, in the seventh year you must let him go free.

Exodus and Deuteronomy seem to state different stipulations regarding the release of the female slave. In Exodus, only the male may go free in the seventh year. In Deuteronomy, that option is open to women.

We should note that these two laws actually do not claim to be addressing exactly the same situation. *Three* women are spoken of in Exodus 21:1–7. The first was *already* married to the male slave at the beginning of the seven-year period. The second was given to the male servant (and bore him children) *after* he became a slave. According to 21:3, the first woman may go free with her husband, but, according to 21:4, the second may not. Exodus 21:7 has yet another woman in mind: a daughter sold into slavery by her father. She has no provision for release. Deuteronomy 15 seems to have yet another scenario in view: any male or female slave who sells himself or herself has the right to go free in the seventh year.

On one level, one can argue that, since Deuteronomy and Exodus have different scenarios in view, this indicates no real tension between them. To a certain extent, this is correct, but these slave laws demonstrate diversity *precisely because they envision different scenarios*. In Deuteronomy, the provision described in Exodus 21:4 (the second woman) does not even come into view. The focus seems to have shifted from specifying *various* circumstances under which male and female slaves *may* (or may not) go free to focusing on *one* scenario where both *must* go free.

It is counterproductive to attempt to reconcile these two laws by arguing that they really say the same thing. They don't. The better question to ask is how to account for these differences. From a historical point of view, that could be done by appealing to Israel's "heightened social consciousness" in Deuteronomy, as some do. As we saw above, we can appeal to the differing historical context of Deuteronomy and suggest that the former law (Exod. 21) needed to be expanded (Deut. 15) in order to assure the grandest measure of magnanimity possible as Israel entered the promised land. (Again, we think here of the motive for the fourth commandment in Deuteronomy focusing on Israel's treatment of its servants as needing to be different from how the Egyptians treated them.) However we might address the matter, the point to be made is simply that there is diversity in the Old Testament in how the question of the release of slaves is to be handled, though all of these texts come to Moses from God and are comfortably in the same canon. To be sure, this can be somewhat unsettling, but these are the facts of the matter. Any discussion of what the Bible is must engage the diversity that the Bible itself exhibits.

Passover

Passover was a central ceremony in ancient Israel. It is rooted in the exodus, where God passed through Egypt and killed every firstborn child. Only those with the blood of the lamb around their doors would be "passed over" (Exod. 12:12–13). After slaughtering the lamb for its blood, the Israelites were to prepare it for the Passover meal:

> That same night they are to eat the meat *roasted* over the fire, along with bitter herbs, and bread made without yeast. *Do not eat the meat raw or cooked in water, but roast it over the fire*—head, legs and inner parts. (Exod. 12:8–9, italics added)

The same law is given again in Deuteronomy 16:5–7, and on the surface the two seem to be in agreement:

> You must not sacrifice the Passover in any town the LORD your God gives you except in the place he will choose as a dwelling for his Name. There you must sacrifice the Passover in the evening, when the sun goes down, on the anniversary of your departure from Egypt. *Roast it and eat it* at

the place the LORD your God will choose. Then in the morning return to your tents. (italics added)

Nothing seems amiss here, but the New International Version actually obscures a problem that in the Hebrew is quite striking. Again, Exodus is very emphatic (the consonants of the Hebrew verbs are given in brackets):

> . . . roasted [ts-l-y] over the fire . . . do not eat the meat raw or cooked [b-sh-l] in water, but roast [ts-l-y] it over the fire.

Deuteronomy actually does not say "roast [ts-l-y] it and eat it" as the New International Version has it, but "boil [b-sh-l] it and eat it." What Exodus says emphatically *not* to do—to boil the meat—is precisely what Deuteronomy says *to* do. Some try to argue (as reflected in the New International Version) that b-sh-l *cannot* mean "boil" but *must* mean "roast" in Deuteronomy 16:7. But in my view this is motivated more by a desire to reconcile these two laws than to understand the relationship between them.

In a way, one can understand why the New International Version handles this problem the way it does. It reflects a translation philosophy rooted in a doctrine of Scripture that the same law cannot be stated in two flatly opposed ways. Yet, there is greater danger in obscuring a linguistic fact to "protect" the Bible, since such problems will eventually come to light and sometimes at the hands of those with little spiritual sensitivity for the larger issues involved. There is a clear difference between these two laws, which is demonstrated by a third passage, 2 Chronicles 35:13:

> They *roasted* [b-sh-l] the Passover animals over the fire as prescribed, and *boiled* [b-sh-l] the holy offerings in pots, caldrons and pans and served them quickly to all the people. (italics added)

Here the topic is once again the Passover meal. The writer of Chronicles seems to be aware of the tensions involved between Exodus and Deuteronomy. In fact, to some scholars, it seems that Chronicles is trying to account for both laws by *combining them into one law*. The New International Version again seems to obscure the Hebrew. Although the New International Version has "roasted," the Hebrew word is once again b-sh-l ("boiled"), not ts-l-y ("roasted"). What we actually read in Chronicles, then, is not that the Israelites "roasted the Passover animals over the fire." That translation does not do justice to the Hebrew text. Rather Chronicles says that they "boiled the Passover animals in the fire." One might ask how you can boil meat in fire: you roast in fire, but boil in water. Yet that is precisely what Chronicles says. It may be, as some scholars suggest, that Chronicles is merging Exodus (roast *in fire*) and Deuteronomy (*boil* in water) by taking elements of both: "boil in fire."

Sacrifice

There is no need to defend the central importance of sacrifice in the Old Testament. Although it is one-sided to suggest that the essence of Israelite religion was defined by sacrifice (especially since all other known ancient religions had a sacrificial system in place as well), there is no question that sacrifice was a nonnegotiable element. The practice was certainly in place well before Mount Sinai. It is assumed as far back as the stories of Cain and Abel (Gen. 4:4) and Abraham (Gen. 15:9–10). Even in Exodus 23:18, before any specific commands were given concerning Israel's obligations to sacrifice, we read:

> Do not offer the blood of a sacrifice to me along with anything containing yeast. The fat of my festival offerings must not be kept until morning.

Even before the specifics of Israel's sacrificial *system* were introduced (Exod. 27:1–8; Lev. 1–7), the Old Testament itself indicates that sacrifice was woven into Israel's fabric from a much earlier time. What happened at Mount Sinai was the *institution* of the *particular* restrictions and obligations concerning sacrifice that would *distinguish* Israelite practices from those of its ancient Near Eastern neighbors.

To choose not to adhere to this system met with dire consequences. The purpose of sacrifice, after all, was to deal with the guilt of the people, that is, to atone for their sin. Even if the people sinned unintentionally, they were guilty and sacrifice had to be made (Lev. 4:13). Not just individuals but kings were to hold to this standard (4:22). They represented the people, and so the consequences of their actions were felt by all. In fact, as we saw earlier, it was the kings' faithfulness to keeping God's law—including the sacrificial system—and leading the people in the observance of God's law that made or broke their reigns. A sacrificial system was put into place in Israel as a means by which Israel (individually and collectively) could remain in fellowship with God and not be "cut off" (e.g., 7:21, 27).

No one would think that sacrifice was optional or that refusing to sacrifice would carry anything other than strict penalties. Still, even in view of the central—even unimpeachable—place that sacrifice held for ancient Israelites, there is a strand in the prophetic literature that adds a dimension to the matter. A well-known passage is Hosea 6:6:

> For I desire mercy, not sacrifice,
>   and acknowledgment of God rather than burnt offerings.

Similar sentiments are found in Amos 5:21–27, Micah 6:6–8, Isaiah 1:11–14, and Jeremiah 7:21–23. Of course, taken in isolation, declarations such as these seem extreme, but it is certain that they were never meant to be taken in isolation. The prophetic critique was not against sacrifice in the abstract—as if the prophets were instigating a total about-face from the law of Moses. They were speaking to the mere institutionalizing of sacrifice, that is, sacrifice without heartfelt obedience in the remainder of one's life. Jeremiah 7:22–23 makes the point clear (the New International Version below adds the word *just* to emphasize this point, but this word is not in the Hebrew text):

> For when I brought your forefathers out of Egypt and spoke to them, I did not [just] give them commands about burnt offerings and sacrifices, but I gave them this command: Obey me, and I will be your God and you will be my people. Walk in all the ways I command you, that it may go well with you.

What is important for us to note, however, is that within the Old Testament itself there is a dynamic quality. Even something so fundamental to Israel's religious system as sacrifice is open to critical reflection. Similar to what we saw with Proverbs, there is no flat teaching of sacrifice in the Old Testament. Rather, biblical voices address the matter of sacrifice in different ways, depending on what the situation demands. To put the matter directly, there is in the Bible a built-in dynamic quality that invites faithful readers to consider the *situation* into which the Bible is being applied. At times, when circumstances are right, even the divine command to sacrifice was set aside in favor of other weightier matters that required attention.

There is no question where Christians today stand on the issue of sacrifice: Christ, the final sacrifice, has come. It is not the case that the gospel displays a flexibility toward the Old Testament command. Quite the opposite. The Old Testament command is fulfilled in the most complete manner possible: the sacrifice of the Son of God. Still, while we are on the topic of the flexibility of the law, it might be helpful to look at how the first Christians handled a similar matter of great legal importance: circumcision.

In Acts 15:5 we read how some Christians insisted that Gentiles must be circumcised in order to be Christians. In a way, one can hardly blame them for voicing such an opinion, since in several places the Old Testament states that to be uncircumcised meant to be outside the family of God (Judg. 15:18; 1 Sam. 14:6; Isa. 52:1; Ezek. 44:7). Yet, despite all this, Paul can say that circumcision amounts to nothing (1 Cor. 7:19) and that insisting on circumcision abolishes "the offense of the cross" (Gal. 5:11). What makes the difference is that Christ has come, and now the circumcision of the heart that the Old Testament speaks of (Deut. 10:16; 30:6) is brought into prominence. As we saw briefly regarding the Sabbath law, the authority of Christ puts an important aspect of the Old Testament into a different focus.

But in this connection what is even more interesting is Acts 16:1–3:

> He came to Derbe and then to Lystra, where a disciple named Timothy lived, whose mother was a Jewess and a believer, but whose father was a Greek. The brothers at Lystra and Iconium spoke well of him. Paul wanted to take him along on the journey, so he circumcised him because of the Jews who lived in that area, for they all knew that his father was a Greek.

Just a few verses after Paul, Barnabas, and Peter all came to the conclusion that circumcision is no longer binding for Gentiles to enter God's family (Acts 15:1–35, esp. 15:2, 10–11, 28–29), we read that Paul has Timothy, a Gentile, circumcised. It was not the case, however, that Paul had temporarily become a Judaizer himself. Rather, Paul does what he does because the *situation* calls for it. The driving concern for Paul is that he and Timothy be able to bear effective witness to the risen Christ in a Jewish context. Paul has Timothy circumcised not in order to save *him*, but so that there would be no unnecessary obstacle for the *Jews* to be saved. In the same way, all law now must submit to the authority of Christ, for it is in Christ that the law is now fulfilled (Matt. 5:17). This leads us to the place of Gentiles in the Old Testament.

Gentiles

Israel was called by God to be a separate ethnic and religious entity, a process that began with the call of Abraham in Genesis 12. Whatever might have been Abraham's previous life, he was now chosen by God to leave his country and become "a great nation" (12:2) through whom "all peoples on earth will be blessed" (12:3).

Already in the story of Abraham we see a tension that will continue to surface throughout the Old Testament: Israel is to think of itself as separate from all other peoples of the world—the Gentiles—while at the same time maintaining some sort of vital connection with them. These are two poles that must be allowed to remain side by side. A good place to see this tension begins in Deuteronomy 23:3:

> No Ammonite or Moabite or any of his descendants may ever enter the assembly of the LORD, even down to the tenth generation. (my translation)

We see here that the Ammonites and Moabites are not permitted *ever* to enter the "assembly of the LORD." The reasons cited in Deuteronomy 23:4–6 are (1) the hostility of these people to the Israelites after they left Egypt and (2) their hiring of Balaam to curse the Israelites (Num. 22–24). They may have had certain rights to dwell within Israel's borders (e.g., Deut. 1:16), but they clearly are not considered as belonging to Israel, being one of them. They are different, and the prohibition against the Ammonites and Moabites is forever binding. In Ezra 9 and Nehemiah 13:1–3, this law in Deuteronomy is repeated and made the basis for the ban against intermarriage.

On the other hand, we have the book of Ruth. Ruth is a Moabitess, yet her first husband, Mahlon, was an Israelite from the tribe of Judah. She later married another Israelite, Boaz, and their child Obed became the ancestor to none other than David himself. There clearly seems to be some flexibility in the binding injunction of Deuteronomy 23:3 against association with Ammonites and Moabites. Further, when we put passages such as Deuteronomy 23:3 side by side with the book of Jonah, where God has a heart of compassion for none other than wicked Nineveh, and Isaiah 19:18–25, where we read of God's plan for, of all people, Egypt, we get a more diverse picture of God's position toward the Gentiles.

But again, the tension is already hinted at in Genesis 12:1–3. We conclude, therefore, that these two sets of passages—those that highlight separation and those that highlight integration—cannot be isolated from each other. In fact, it is precisely by being a separate people that Israel can eventually be used by God as a vehicle to bless "all peoples on earth." By first learning obedience, being a faithful witness to God in the world, the Israelites would shine as "a light for the Gentiles" in order to bring "salvation to the ends of the earth" (Isa. 49:6). To speak this way is certainly not to suggest a fundamental contradiction between these two attitudes toward the Gentiles. It is, rather, to recognize that the Old Testament is not a flat book where all parts agree on a superficial level. How does God feel about the Israelites and their relationship with the Gentiles? That depends on what passage in the Old Testament you are reading.

There is coherence between the parts, but that coherence transcends the level of simple statements or propositions. It is to be found precisely in the unfolding drama of Israel and the world, where the nature of Israel's relationship to the Gentiles develops over time. We must look at Scripture as a story moving in a certain direction. Christians believe that the story reaches its climax in the person and work of Christ, where Jew and Gentile finally become one people of God, united together in the crucified and risen Christ (Gal. 3:26–29). It is in Christ, the true and faithful Israelite, that "Israel" can finally become a light to the Gentiles, bringing salvation to all the earth. But the climactic force of such an event can be fully appreciated only by allowing the diverse voices of the Old Testament, right from the beginning, to have their say, unhindered by efforts to reconcile them to each other.

Although we have looked at many laws in detail, we should not get lost in those details. We must take a step back and view the big picture: diversity in the Old Testament exists, even on the level of the legal data. We can now move to two final examples of diversity in the Old Testament that concern God himself.

God and Diversity

One God or Many Gods?

It is considered fundamental to the Old Testament that Israel's God is the one and only God. He alone is the creator of the world and the sustainer of Israel. There are no others gods. Idols that the other nations worship are mere blocks of wood and stone. Such thinking put Israel's faith on a collision course with that of the surrounding nations, all of whom worshiped a multiplicity of gods. My intention here is not to call this belief into question. What I am interested in, however, is discussing *how* the Old Testament speaks of the existence of one God in the context of the religious systems of the surrounding nations. It is even here, in this most fundamental of beliefs, that we find some diversity in the Old Testament witness.

Several key passages in the Old Testament speak of Yahweh alone as God. In Isaiah 44:6–20, Isaiah mocks the gods of Babylon. Whereas Israel's God predicts the future (44:8), Babylon's gods are mere idols made of stone and wood (44:12–20). Jeremiah expresses a similar notion in Jeremiah 10:1–16. Idols do not create, nor do they have the power to save. They are merely fashioned by people out of lumps of stone and wood. In 1 Kings 18:16–46, Elijah confronts the prophets of **Baal** and **Asherah**, well-known male and female gods, respectively, in the ancient Near East, whose popularity has been confirmed by archeological discoveries. Such popular religious practice was an ever-present temptation for Israel, a fact demonstrated by the frequency with which the Old Testament prophets denounce Israel for its lapse into Baal/Asherah worship.

Elijah's challenge to the prophets of Baal and Asherah is to put up or shut up. As the story goes, the prophets of Baal and Asherah dance themselves into a frenzy—including slashing themselves with swords and spears—in an effort to get their gods to ignite the altar. Elijah's God, however, ignites the altar with fire from heaven, even after it has been soaked three times with water. The demonstration has the desired effect: "When all the people saw this, they fell prostrate and cried, 'The LORD—he is God! The LORD—he is God!'" (1 Kings 18:39). The Canaanite gods were shown to be no gods after all.

All this is true, and I am not deflecting the force of this central biblical doctrine. But my point is that the Old Testament paints a more varied portrait of God. There is enough biblical evidence to suggest that Israel's understanding that Yahweh alone is God must be understood within the context of the polytheistic cultures of the ancient Near East (i.e., belief in the existence of many gods). The passages we glimpsed in Isaiah, Jeremiah, and 1 Kings represent high mountain peaks in an overall terrain that is much more rugged.

To put the matter this way is to take very seriously the *historical* realities of Israel's existence. It may be helpful here to recall what we saw in chapter 2. Our focus there was on how the ancient Near Eastern environment could help us understand the opening chapters of Genesis. Abraham, the first Israelite, was a Mesopotamian, born and raised in a polytheistic society. It is important here that we not allow our own modern sensitivities to influence how we understand Israel's ancient faith. *We* may not believe that multiple gods ever existed, but *ancient Near Eastern people* did. This is the religious world within which God called Israel to be his people. When God called Israel, he *began* leading them into a full knowledge of who he is, but he started where they were.

We should not be surprised, therefore, when we see the Old Testament describe God as *greater than* the gods of the surrounding nations. In the Psalms, for example, this is seen in a number of passages:

> *Among the gods* there is none like you, O Lord;
>   no deeds can compare with yours. (86:8)

> For the LORD is the great God,
>   the great King *above all gods*. (95:3)

> For great is the LORD and most worthy of praise;
>   he is to be *feared above all gods*. (96:4)

> For you, O Lord, are the Most High over all the earth;
>   you are exalted far *above all gods*. (97:9)

> I know that the Lord is great,
>   that our Lord is *greater than all gods*. (135:5)

> Give thanks to the *God of gods*.
>   His love endures forever. (136:2)

I suppose one could argue that the psalmists were just writing "poetry" and didn't really intend to be taken literally. On the other hand, the point of the comparison is to exalt Yahweh by way of contrast. For the comparison to have any real punch, both entities must be *presumed* to be real. For example, we may tell our children something like, "Don't be afraid of the dark. God is greater than the Boogey Man." Of course, adults who say this know that the Boogey Man is not real, but they know that their *children* believe he is real. Even in contemporary Christian expression, we compare God to many things: our problems, our challenges, our enemies, and so on. And each comparison is made between two real (or perceived to be real) entities. This is what these psalms are doing as well. Even though Isaiah, Jeremiah, and 1 Kings seem to make a very different point—that other gods do not exist—and even certain psalms take up that point (e.g., 4:2; 40:4; 106:28), that should not drive us to dismiss the witness of these other psalms as being of secondary importance, nor should we succumb to the temptation to interpret these psalms in a way that is compatible with what we "know" to be true. Rather, we must let all of Scripture have its say and be willing to compose as diverse a portrait of God as the biblical data demand.

Along a similar line, Joshua 24:2, 14–15 is interesting:

> Joshua said to all the people, "This is what the Lord, the God of Israel, says: 'Long ago your forefathers, including Terah the father of Abraham and Nahor, lived beyond the River and worshiped other gods. . . .'
>
> "Now fear the Lord and serve him with all faithfulness. Throw away the gods your forefathers worshiped beyond the River and in Egypt, and serve the Lord. But if serving the Lord seems undesirable to you, then choose for yourselves this day whom you will serve, whether the gods your forefathers served beyond the River, or the gods of the Amorites, in whose land you are living. But as for me and my household, we will serve the Lord."

Joshua is exhorting Israel to serve Yahweh *alone*. To serve him alone means *not* to serve other gods. They are to do now what their father Abraham had done before: although he once worshiped other gods, he turned from them. We do not have here the more dramatic kind of state-ment we find in Isaiah or Jeremiah. Joshua's point here is not that there *are* no other gods, but that Yahweh *alone* is worthy of worship. Joshua is not providing the Israelites with a bare statement of monotheism. He is making the case to Israel—a case that in the polytheistic world of the ancient Near East is itself very drastic—that, among all the gods, Yahweh is the God they should serve. The reason they should serve him alone is that *Yahweh*, not some other god, is the one who brought them out of Egypt and into the land (see Josh. 24:5–13, and esp. 24:16–18).

We see a similar idea in the book of Exodus. When Moses and Aaron go to confront Pharaoh, they say, "Let my people go, so that they may hold a festival to me in the desert" (Exod. 5:1). Pharaoh's response is telling:

> Who is the LORD, that I should obey him and let Israel go? I do not know the LORD and I will not let Israel go. (5:2)

Moses and Aaron respond:

> The God of the Hebrews has met with us. Now let us take a three-day journey into the desert to offer sacrifices to the LORD our God, or he may strike us with plagues or with the sword. (5:3)

Moses and Aaron demand that Pharaoh allow the Israelites to worship their God in the desert. But Pharaoh does not know who Yahweh is. The next several chapters, culminating in the Red Sea incident, are designed to acquaint Pharaoh and all Egypt with Israel's God. This purpose is made explicit in 9:15–16, a statement found in the middle of the plague narrative:

> For by now I could have stretched out my hand and struck you and your people with a plague that would have wiped you off the earth. But I have raised you up for this very purpose, that I might show you my power and that my name might be proclaimed in all the earth.

The plagues are not just displays of God's power in the abstract. They are declarations of war against the power structure of Egypt, founded upon the myriad of Egyptian gods. The plagues bear witness to Egypt and Israel that Israel's God is not just mightier than Pharaoh, but mightier than the gods that Pharaoh and his people serve. The plagues and the final blow at the Red Sea were an argument to all that Yahweh alone is worthy of worship, not the gods of mighty Egypt. In fact, some of the plagues are thought to reflect elements of the Egyptian pantheon:

- Plague 1, Nile turns to blood: The Nile was personified and worshiped in Egypt. God turned it to blood.
- Plague 2, frogs from the Nile: Heqet, the Egyptian goddess of childbirth, was depicted in Egyptian art with the head of a frog. Later, God will kill Egypt's firstborn.
- Plague 5, death to livestock: Hathor, the mother and sky goddess, was depicted as a cow.
- Plague 7, hail: A hailstorm, accompanied by thunder and "fire" (likely lightning; see Exod. 9:23), shows Yahweh's supremacy over Egyptian gods associated with storms (e.g., Seth).
- Plague 9, darkness: The Egyptian sun god was Re (sometimes spelled Ra), and Pharaoh was considered his son or earthly representative. God blocks him out to make it dark during the day.
- Plague 10, death of the firstborn: Osiris was the Egyptian god of the dead, yet Yahweh will claim the firstborn as his own.

We must remember that the Israelites had spent generations as slaves living and working in the polytheistic world of Egypt. That was the world they knew. Now God was about to bring them out of that world and carry them off to another—the land of Canaan, which was as much a polytheistic culture as any other. What would have spoken to these Israelites—what would have met them where they were—was not a declaration of monotheism (belief that only one God exists), out of the blue. Their ears would not have been prepared to hear that. What we read in Exodus is perhaps less satisfying for us, but it would have set the ancient world on its head: this god Yahweh, who lives in a desert, who is a god of slaves, who no one had even heard of before, meets these powerful Egyptian gods on their own turf, and—if I may put it this way—beats them up.

This brings us to the opening of the Ten Commandments. They begin with a prologue (as we saw in chapter 2): "I am the LORD your God, who brought you out of Egypt, out of the land of slavery" (Exod. 20:2). This prologue establishes the basis for the commandments: what God has done. Delivering the Israelites from Egypt gives God the right to command that they worship him in the way he is about to outline. The first commandment reads: "You shall have no other gods before me" (20:3). Modern readers might be tempted to add, "But of course, as we all know, there *are* no other gods." But this is not what the text says or implies, and we must resist the temptation to assume that ancient Israelites had at their disposal what we do: a fuller revelation of God. The first commandment says not "There *are* no other gods" but "You *shall have* no other gods." Yahweh is saying, "You saw what *I* did in bringing you up from Egypt. Now, *I* am the one you are to worship, not the gods of Egypt you are leaving behind nor the gods of Canaan you are about to encounter."

This reading of the first commandment may be counterintuitive for contemporary Christians, but that is precisely the point. If we wish to understand ancient Israelites and the ancient literature they composed, we must learn to develop intuitions, as best we can, that reflect the ancient world to which these texts were given.

We see the same point made in the second commandment:

> You shall not make for yourself an idol in the form of anything in heaven above or on the earth beneath or in the waters below. You shall not bow down to them or worship them; for I, the LORD your God, am a jealous God, punishing the children for the sin of the fathers to the third and fourth generation of those who hate me, but showing love to a thousand generations of those who love me and keep my commandments. (20:4–6)

The way this commandment is phrased seems to imply that idols can be real rivals of Yahweh, so much so that he would be *jealous* if Israel were to worship them. Again, remember that, standing as we are with the benefit of much subsequent revelation and reflection, we *know* that idols are not real. We also know that *anything* other than God, if it becomes an object of devotion (spouse, career, money, fame), is an idol. But the Israelites of the exodus were living in the infancy of their national existence amid a polytheistic world. They were taking their first baby steps toward a knowledge of God that later generations came to understand and we perhaps take for granted. At this point in the progress of redemption, however, the gods of the surrounding nations are treated as real. God shows his absolute supremacy over them by declaring not that "they don't exist" but that "they cannot stand up against me—look at what I did in Egypt. Did the gods of Egypt help you? No. I did it. And when you enter Canaan and you are met with a whole new list of gods, remember: *I* brought you out of Egypt. What I did to their gods I will do to any other gods who get between you and me. Do not worship them."

To read the plagues and the first and second commandments this way makes good sense in Israel's historical moment. And it should cause no difficulty for us if we remember that God always speaks in ways that the people understand, not simply to leave them there but to bring them along to deeper knowledge of himself. And that process does not come to completion until God reveals himself in a very material way—not in an idol made of stone or wood, but in flesh and blood. There is no image by which God is to be worshiped other than the image he himself fashioned—his own incarnation.

Does God Change His Mind?

Every Christian knows instinctively, and correctly, that God is not a part of creation. He is the creator and therefore separate from his creation. Obviously that does not mean that he does not take part in his creation. From beginning to end, the Bible is a story of God's involvement in the affairs of humanity. (In fact, this truth is the foundation for this entire book.) But he is still supreme *over* his creation, meaning that he is not part of the created order and that he does not need creation in any way to be complete. Many well-known biblical images come to mind that speak to this portrait of God: creator, deliverer, mighty one, king, father, warrior, potter. These all say that God is in control, he does as he wishes (although not haphazardly or unjustly), no one can stop what he determines to do, and any such attempts are simply foolish rebellion.

Yet, in various places in the Old Testament, God acts more as a character in the story. Another way of putting it is that he acts more humanlike than godlike. This is especially true of narrative portions of the Old Testament. One example is the binding of Isaac in Genesis 22. At God's command, Abraham sets out to sacrifice his son Isaac. At the last moment, God intervenes to stop Abraham from plunging the knife into his son.

> "Do not lay a hand on the boy," he [the angel] said. "Do not do anything to him. Now I know that you fear God, because you have not withheld from me your son, your only son." (Gen. 22:12)

Abraham was tested by God. It is clear that the purpose of the test was not to prove anything to Abraham but to God. For God to say "Now I know" makes sense *in this story* only if the test was a *real* test; if something was at stake. It was on the basis of Abraham passing the test that God said "*Now* I know." *In this story*, God did not know until after the test was passed.

Another example concerns the cause of the flood as explained in Genesis 6:5–8:

> The LORD saw how great man's wickedness on the earth had become, and that every inclination of the thoughts of his heart was only evil all the time. The LORD was grieved that he had made man on the earth, and his heart was filled with pain. So the LORD said, "I will wipe mankind, whom I have created, from the face of the earth—men and animals, and creatures that move along the ground, and birds of the air—for I am grieved that I have made them." But Noah found favor in the eyes of the LORD.

The flow of this story clearly implies that God is *reacting* to the wickedness described in Genesis 6:1–4. It is *because of* the cohabitation of the "sons of God" and "daughters of men" (the identity of these figures has been a problem for biblical interpreters since before Christ and won't detain us here) that God is grieved. This is such a grievous turn of events that God is even willing to undo his own creation.

The scene is straightforward: (1) God creates everything good; (2) wickedness and evil enter; (3) God *reacts* by intending to wipe out everything he made. Of course, it is possible to say that God already anticipated step 3 in step 1, that is, he knew what was going to happen, and so step 2 does not take him by surprise. That may be so, but that is only a guess that goes far beyond what we read. The story is told in such a way that steps 2 and 3 have an unexpected quality to them. Any attempt to force the God *of Genesis 6* into a mold cast by certain theological commitments or to reconcile this description to other biblical passages simply amounts to reading past this story. I take it as a fundamental truth, however, that God did not put this story here so we could read past it.

A third example concerns the golden calf incident in Exodus 32–34. After leaving Egypt and seeing God's glory on Mount Sinai, the Israelites do the unthinkable: they build an idol, a golden calf. In doing so, they break at least the second commandment (make no idols) and perhaps also the first (if the calf is an image of Yahweh—and it may be—then, technically, the first commandment has not been broken). God intends to wipe out the Israelites and start over with Moses (32:10). But Moses intervenes and appeals to God's sense of honor to follow through with his promise to Abraham to make his descendants numerous:

> But Moses sought the favor of the LORD his God. "O LORD," he said, "why should your anger burn against your people, whom you brought out of Egypt with great power and a mighty hand? Why should the Egyptians say, 'It was with evil intent that he brought them out, to kill them in the mountains and to wipe them off the face of the earth'? Turn from your fierce anger; relent and do not bring disaster on your people. Remember your servants Abraham, Isaac and Israel, to whom you swore by your own self: 'I will make your descendants as numerous as the stars in the sky and I will give your descendants all this land I promised them, and it will be their inheritance forever.'" Then the LORD relented and did not bring on his people the disaster he had threatened. (Exod. 32:11–14)

Moses' appeal works: turn, relent, do not bring disaster, remember. He reminds God of his own promises to Israel's first ancestors (see 2:24–25) and in doing so *convinces* God not to do what he had earlier (32:10) said he would do. Hence, *in this narrative*, God changes his mind.

In 32:35, God punishes those Israelites who had sinned (see 32:33). Yet, the sin was so great that, although he is now allowing them to enter Canaan, he refuses to accompany them:

> Go up to the land flowing with milk and honey. But I will not go with you, because you are a stiff-necked people and I might destroy you on the way. (33:3)

Then in 33:5 God says,

> You are a stiff-necked people. If I were to go with you even for a moment, I might destroy you. Now take off your ornaments and I will decide what to do with you.

God is saying, "I won't go with you. You don't want me to go with you. You don't know what I might do. *I* don't know what I might do." In 33:15–16, Moses counters by appealing to God's obligation to follow through with his plan to make Israel a special nation:

> Then Moses said to him, "If your Presence does not go with us, do not send us up from here. How will anyone know that you are pleased with me and with your people unless you go with us? What else will distinguish me and your people from all the other people on the face of the earth?"

The Lord responds:

> I will do the very thing you have asked, because I am pleased with you and I know you by name. (33:17)

Moses gets God to change his plans again.

More examples could be discussed. In fact, from one perspective, the entire narrative structure of the Old Testament is fueled by the back and forth, give and take between God and Israel. The Old Testament *portrays* God as a being who can be acted upon, a being whose actions are in a meaningful sense of the word contingent upon what his people do: *if* they obey, *then* God will bless; *if* they disobey, *then* God will curse. I am well aware that from a philosophical point of view, one can answer this quite simply by saying that God may *act* as if his actions are contingent, but in *reality* they are not. My concern, however, is with *the Bible* and what it says, with how God *acts* in Scripture. I am not at all comfortable with describing God in a way that leads me to dismiss this dimension of how God himself wishes to be known.

I am taking some time to lay out this issue, because, as I write this, a current theological debate in evangelical Christianity concerns the so-called openness of God. Much of that debate centers on whether God controls future events, whether there are possible future events of which God has no knowledge, and even whether God himself is open to change. A focus of that discussion invariably turns to some of the Old Testament passages we have looked at above, passages where God changes his mind.

Despite appearances, what I am addressing here is not immediately relevant to that debate. I am not interested in asking whether God can or cannot change his mind as some abstract discussion. The issue I am addressing is how the Old Testament *describes* God. To ask in the abstract what God can or cannot do is interesting—sort of like "Can God make a rock so big that even he can't lift it?"—but beyond the scope of this book and maybe even beyond the scope of the Bible. It is not the God *behind* the scenes that I want to look at, but the God *of* the scenes, the God of the Bible, how he is portrayed there.

I realize this raises some questions. Does not God, as he is *portrayed* in the Bible, correspond to the God "behind the scenes"? In other words, does not the Bible, because it is the word of God, give us an *accurate* presentation of what God is *really* like? After all, if you drive a wedge between what the Old Testament says about God and what God is *really* like, how can we speak meaningfully of the Bible as God's authoritative word?

This is a very good cluster of questions. I am not trying to drive a wedge between the Bible and God. Actually, and somewhat ironically, this is what I see others doing. I feel bound to talk about God *in the way(s) the Bible does*, even if I am not comfortable with it. The Bible really does have authority if we let it speak, and not when we—intentionally or unintentionally—suspend what the Bible says about God in some places while we work out our speculations about what God is "really" like, perhaps by accenting other portions of the Bible that are more amenable to our thinking. God gave us the Bible so we could read *it*, not so we can ferret our way *behind* it to see how things really are.

God reveals himself *throughout* the Old Testament. There is no part that gets it "more right" than others. Rather, they get at different sides of God. Or, to use the well-worn analogy, the different descriptions of God in the Old Testament are like the different colors and textures that *together* combine to make a portrait. In keeping with the incarnational analogy, we can appreciate that the *entire* Bible, through and through, has that human dimension. So, for the Old Testament to speak of God as changing his mind means that this is *his* choice for how *he* wants us to know him. He speaks about himself in ways that reflect our ability to understand. I might add at this juncture that Christian prayer, which is often expressed as *pleading* before God, operates on the assumption that our words will have some *effect* on God. But do they really? That is for God to know, not us. But many of us have seen enough examples of answers to prayer in the face of a life-threatening illness and dire financial problems to admit that there is a ring of truth to all this.

There are diverse portrayals of God in the Old Testament. He is, on the one hand, powerful, one who knows things before they happen and who causes things to happen, one who is in complete control. On the other hand, he finds things out, he can feel grieved about things that happen, he changes his mind. If we allow either of these dimensions to override the other, we set aside part of God's word in an effort to defend him, which is somewhat of a self-contradiction. But as we think about God, as we learn of him more and more, as we enter deeper into relationship with him through Christ, we will see that there is much in the full-orbed biblical portrait of God that we need to know. And of course, this is no surprise, for this is what he intended. As Paul says, "*All scripture* is . . . profitable" (2 Tim. 3:16 RSV)—even parts that don't fit easily into our molds.

What Does Diversity Tell Us about Scripture?

The types of things reviewed in this chapter can no doubt be somewhat unsettling for some, and I hope I presented the issue in a constructive manner. It seems that there is a significant strand of contemporary Christian thinking on the Old Testament that feels that these sorts of things just shouldn't happen. And, if they do, they just *appear* to be a problem. You just need to read a bit more closely or do a little more research, and if you're patient enough, you'll get the right answer eventually. For others, however (including myself), such an approach comes close to intellectual dishonesty. To accept the diversity of the Old Testament is not to "cave in to liberalism," nor is it to seek after novelty. It is, rather, to read the Old Testament quite honestly and seriously. And if diversity is such a prevalent phenomenon in the Old Testament, it would seem to be important to do more than simply take note of diversity and file it away for future reference. We must ask why God would do it *this* way. Why does God's word look the way it does?

On one level, there is no final answer to this question; no answer can be given that would close off all further discussion. But we can make some observations to point us in the right direction. For one thing, it is important to reiterate that diversity is not imposed on the Bible, nor are recent generations the first to take note of this. It is part of Scripture's fabric, and the two-thousand-year history of Jewish and Christian interpretation bears witness to this. We have even seen one example where the Bible itself seems to be taking account of its own diversity (the Passover law in 2 Chron. 35:13). As I said at the beginning of this chapter, for modern evangelicalism the tendency is to move toward a defensive or apologetic handling of the biblical evidence, to protect the Bible against the modernist charge that diversity is evidence of errors in the Bible and, consequently, that the Bible is not inspired by God. Unfortunately, this legacy accepts the worldview offered by modernity and defends the Bible by a rational standard that the Bible itself challenges rather than acknowledges. This contributes to the stress that some Christians feel in trying to maintain an evangelical faith while at the same time trying to give honest answers to difficult questions.

Is the fact of diversity fundamentally contrary to the Bible being the word of God? My answer is no. And the way in which we can begin to address this issue is to confess *at the outset*, along with the historic Christian church, that the Bible *is* the word of God. That is our starting point, a confession of faith, not creating a standard of what the Bible *should* look like and then assessing the Bible on the basis of that standard. If we begin with the confession that the Bible is God's word, that it ultimately comes from him, that it is what the Spirit of God wanted it to be, that there is no place in all the messiness of the Old Testament where God says, "Oops, I didn't really mean to put it that way—I'd like to try again, please"—if we begin there, we have the freedom to look honestly and deeply at what God is doing in the Bible.

In other words, once we confess *that* the Bible is God's word, we can look at *how* it is God's word. That investigation will not come to an end in this life. There is always a freshness and inscrutability about the Bible. This goes hand in hand with believing that the Bible is God's word; it will always be bigger than what we can comprehend. There is always more thinking and reflection to be done in observing how Scripture behaves and what conclusions we can draw.

What the diversity of the Bible tells us is that there is no superficial unity to the Bible. Portions of the Bible are in tension with each other, as we have seen. *That* these tensions exist is a matter of simple observation. A better question is *why* they exist and what this tells us about the nature of Scripture and, by extension, the nature of God. One thing that such tensions demonstrate to us is how fully God participates in history, that he *incarnates* himself throughout Israel's history. From this perspective, it is to be expected that the Old Testament exhibits significant diversity. After all, it was written over a very lengthy period of time, at least five hundred years and perhaps closer to one thousand years. And the history it covers spans from creation to the postexilic period. Discounting the primeval history (Gen. 1–11), there is still roughly a fifteen-hundred-year span of time between the time of Israel's earliest ancestors and the return of Israel's southern kingdom from exile in Babylon. What is true of any historical study covering a similar time span is also true of ancient Israel and its place in the ancient Near East: during this time cultures, worldviews, political alliances, and so on shifted, changed, developed.

If we take seriously both the historical dimension of Israel's story and God's making himself a part of that story, one would expect this complex historical matrix to be reflected in the pages of the Old Testament, which is precisely what we find. The various books of the Old Testament were written in differing historical contexts and for different purposes. This is why, as we have seen, Samuel–Kings and Chronicles can look so different from each other while talking about the same things. And not only are there different historical periods to take into account, but different genres of literature as well. The wisdom sayings of Proverbs are not the same type of literature as the Psalms, which are themselves not the same type as law, which is very different from historical narratives.

With all this variety in historical context, purpose, and genre, variety in *content* should be one of the first things we expect to see in the Old Testament. "But surely not the Bible," one might say. "The Bible is from God. It must be consistent, unified. Whatever we might be able to say about *other* types of ancient books, the Bible is a message to be proclaimed, not a loose collection of diverse theological points of view. After all, God would not want to confuse us like that." But such a line of reasoning serves only to detach the Old Testament and God himself from the world into which it first spoke. To do so is to brush aside the fundamental notion of revelation discussed in chapter 2: *for God to reveal himself means that he accommodates himself.* To be understood, he condescends to the conventions and conditions of those to whom he is revealing himself. The word of God cannot be kept safe from the rough-and-tumble drama of human history. For the Bible to be the word of God implies the exact opposite.

I suspect that one reason this causes problems for some is not because of what it says about Scripture, but what it implies about God. What kind of a God would "do it *this* way"? But surely the answer is that it shows us a God who goes very low to know his people and to make himself known. The messiness of the Old Testament, which is a source of embarrassment for some, is actually a positive. On one level it may not help with a certain brand of apologetics, where we use the so-called perfection of the Bible to prove to nonbelievers that Christianity is true. But this method is as wrongheaded as it is to argue that Christianity is true by downplaying the humanness of Christ. Also, we must remember that the Bible is a book for the people of God. It is not an evangelistic tract, designed to convert nonbelievers (although the Holy Spirit certainly uses the Bible this way!). It is a book written for those who are part of God's family. In that context, the messiness of the Old Testament tells *us* that God is very real to his people and very near.

Can Christians speak of a unity to the Bible? Yes, but it is not a superficial unity based on the surface content of the words of passages taken in isolation. The unity of the Bible is more subtle but at the same time deeper. It is a unity that should ultimately be sought in Christ himself, the living word. This itself is not a superficial unity, as if we can "find Jesus" in every passage of the Old Testament (a point we will address from a different angle in the next chapter). It is, rather, a broad and foundational theological commitment based on the analogy between Christ and Scripture.

As Christians we must remember that we believe not only that the *Bible* is the word of God, but that *Christ* himself is the word. What exactly does it mean to refer to Jesus as "the word" (as John does in 1:1–2 of his Gospel)? This could be answered in many ways, but I want to pick up on just one dimension: the Bible is God's word in written form; Christ is God's word in human form. This may sound like so much theological double-talk, but it is in fact a fundamental confession of the historic Christian church, and there is payoff for our topic here. The written word bears witness to the incarnate word, Christ. And what gives the written word its unity is not simply the words on the page, but the incarnate word who is more than simply the sum of the biblical parts. He is the one through whom heaven and earth—including the Bible itself—were created, and he is the one in whom Israel's story reaches its climax. The Bible bears witness to Christ *by Christ's design*. He is over the Bible, beyond it, separate from it, even though the Bible is *his* word and thus bears witness to him.

Christ is supreme, and it is in him, the embodied word, that the written word ultimately finds its unity. Christ is the final destiny of Israel's story, and it is to him that the Bible as a whole bears witness. As Christians, this is our theoretical starting point. This does *not* make all the tensions evaporate before our eyes. Rather, because we know that in Christ Scripture coheres, he is the proper starting point from which to view and respect these tensions. The tensions of the Old Testament should be seen within the context of the Christian Bible as a whole, where Christ—his life, death, resurrection, and ascension—is given the focus he deserves. To put it another way, if, as Christians say, Christ is the focus of Scripture, we should allow that focus to come into play in how we understand Scripture.

Christ is the ultimate example of how God enters the messiness of history to save his people. He did not keep his distance, but became one of us. This is true of Christ, the embodied word. It is also true of the Bible, the written word. To put it this way is to turn the entire debate on its head: the diversity of Scripture—and the tensions that this diversity introduces—bears witness to God's revelation rather than detracts from it.

Further Reading

Alexander, T. Desmond, and Brian S. Rosner. *New Dictionary of Biblical Theology*. Leicester, England: Inter-Varsity; Downers Grove, IL: InterVarsity, 2000.

> Many helpful essays on biblical theology, some of which engage the issue of theological diversity, particularly the introduction.

Barton, John. "Unity and Diversity in the Biblical Canon." Pages 11–26 in *The Unity of Scripture and the Diversity of the Canon*. Edited by J. Barton and M. Wolter. Berlin: de Gruyter, 2003.

> Reviews various approaches to diversity in the Bible. Diversity is not a problem but a virtue in that it functions as a "check on authoritarianism."

Brueggemann, Walter. *Theology of the Old Testament: Testimony, Dispute, Advocacy*. Minneapolis: Fortress, 1997.

> Brueggemann handles the theological diversity of the Old Testament by organizing it under four headings: Israel's core testimony, countertestimony, unsolicited testimony, and embodied testimony. The point is that there are theological countervoices in the Old Testament. This is a fairly recent book, and it remains to be seen how widely accepted Brueggemann's approach will become, but it is helpful in outlining the issue.

Fox, Michael V. *A Time to Tear Down and a Time to Build Up: A Rereading of Ecclesiastes*. Grand Rapids: Eerdmans, 1999.

> Recent commentary that covers many of the issues of theological diversity in Ecclesiastes. For Fox, the contradictions in Ecclesiastes are the heart of the book's theology.

Goldingay, John. *Models for Interpretation of Scripture*. Grand Rapids: Eerdmans, 1995.

> Interacts with the effect that diversity should have on a doctrine of Scripture. The four models for interpreting Scripture reflect the diverse forms that Scripture itself takes: narrative, law, prophecy, and wisdom. Goldingay deals with many of the issues discussed above.

————. *Theological Diversity and the Authority of the Old Testament*. Grand Rapids: Eerdmans, 1987.

> Without a doubt the place to start to see the issues involved in the theological diversity of the Old Testament.

Hanson, Paul D. *The Diversity of Scripture: A Theological Interpretation*. Philadelphia: Fortress, 1982.

> Hanson argues that diversity is built into Scripture (what he calls the form/reform or the visionary/pragmatic polarity). Such diversity, Hanson argues, means that the Bible is a "living force" rather than a "straightjacket of a closed orthodoxy."

Hasel, Gerhard F. *Old Testament Theology: Basic Issues in the Current Debate*. 4th ed. Grand Rapids: Eerdmans, 1991.

> Focuses on the problems involved in doing biblical theology, particularly the question of whether we can speak of a center to the Old Testament in view of the diverse and progressive development of the Old Testament.

Japhet, Sarah. *The Ideology of the Book of Chronicles and Its Place in Biblical Thought*. Frankfurt: Peter Lang, 1989.

> Scholarly treatment of the theological (i.e., ideological) distinctives of Chronicles.

Ward, Timothy. "The Diversity and Sufficiency of Scripture." Pages 192–218 in *The Trustworthiness of God: Perspectives on the Nature of Scripture*. Edited by P. Helm and C. R. Trueman. Grand Rapids: Eerdmans, 2002.

> The diversity of Scripture "both authorizes and chastens any theological endeavor" (218). It makes us "humble and hopeful" (217) in our Christian lives and in our theological formulations.

4

The Old Testament and Its Interpretation in the New Testament

Do New Testament Authors Misuse the Old Testament?

You're sitting in church and the preacher turns to Genesis 31:22 and reads, "On the third day Laban was told that Jacob had fled." The preacher then explains that this verse refers to the resurrection of Christ, since he rose from the dead "on the third day" and "fled" from the grave.

Overall, the sermon was quite edifying, even powerful. Many people were obviously moved to commit their lives to the gospel. Still, you found the preacher's handling of the text to be odd, idiosyncratic—even irresponsible. Your instincts tell you that this passage really has nothing to do with Christ's resurrection. And the context of Genesis 31:22 shows that this is part of a larger story of Jacob running way from his father-in-law Laban and then being pursued by Laban for seven days (31:23). In your wildest imagination, you would never see any connection whatsoever between 31:22 and Christ's resurrection.

This example may strike one as a bit ridiculous, but such things do happen. It is a common occurrence for preachers to take a verse from the Old Testament, or part of a verse, and derive meaning from it that serves their agenda rather than clarifying the text. Instinctively we recoil from such interpretive negligence. We know that to understand the Old Testament (or nearly any human communication, for that matter), the original context and the author's intention should be respected.

I affirm this basic instinct. Even as I write this book, I want to be sure that what I write will be clear, that readers will understand what I am trying to say. What has been a recurring problem, however, for many Christians is how the New Testament authors themselves handled the Old Testament. This phenomenon is somewhat troubling, for it seems to run counter to the instinct that context and authorial intention are the basis for sound interpretation. To observe how the New Testament authors handle the Old Testament is to conclude that their notions of what constitutes a proper handling of the Old Testament do not always square with our own instincts—in fact, quite often, the differences are striking.

Perhaps one example will illustrate. In Luke 20:27–40 (see also Matt. 22:23–33; Mark 12:18–27), Jesus is debating some Sadducees (who do not believe in the resurrection; Luke 20:27) concerning the resurrection of the dead. They come to him with what they feel is a clever argument: if a woman is widowed and remarries seven times, who would be considered her husband at the resurrection? In answering the Sadducees, Jesus appeals to Exodus 3:6 (in italic type below):

> Jesus replied, "The people of this age marry and are given in marriage. But those who are considered worthy of taking part in that age and in the resurrection from the dead will neither marry nor be given in marriage, and they can no longer die; for they are like the angels. They are God's children, since they are children of the resurrection. But in the account of the bush, even Moses showed that the dead rise, for he calls the Lord *the God of Abraham, and the God of Isaac, and the God of Jacob.* He is not the God of the dead, but of the living, for to him all are alive." (Luke 20:34–38)

But when we look at the context of Exodus 3:6, it is hard to see how the Old Testament passage could have been intended to be used as a proof-text for the resurrection. No one reading Exodus and coming across 3:6 would think that resurrection was suddenly the topic of conversation. There God is simply announcing himself to Moses as the God of his ancestors, the God of Abraham, Isaac, and Jacob. The manner in which Jesus uses Exodus 3:6 is striking to our ears. In a way, it is similar to the hypothetical example at the beginning of this chapter: there is no persuasive connection between that passage and how Jesus uses it.

But, no matter how unappealing this use of the Old Testament is for *our* eyes, it seems to have served its purpose for Jesus' audience. As we read in Luke 20:39–40: "Some of the teachers of the law responded, 'Well said, teacher!' And no one dared ask him any more questions." This response of Jesus' listeners is a very important piece of information. That *they* found Jesus' use of the Old Testament to be persuasive is an indication to us that our first order of business is to *understand* the **hermeneutical** (i.e., interpretive) conventions of *their* time *before* we pass judgment.

There are three popular options in evangelical scholarship for addressing the odd manner in which the New Testament authors use the Old Testament:

1. To argue, wherever possible, that the New Testament authors, despite appearances, were actually respecting the context of the Old Testament text they are citing. Although it may not be obvious to us, there must be some *legitimate* trigger in the Old Testament text, since no inspired writer would handle the Old Testament so irresponsibly. Careful examination will reveal that the New Testament's use of the Old Testament text is actually based in and is consistent with that Old Testament author's intention.

2. To concede that the New Testament author is not using the Old Testament text in a manner in which it was intended, but then to say that the New Testament author himself does not intend to "interpret" the text, only "apply" it. Since the New Testament does not intend to present us with hermeneutical models for how it handles the Old Testament, it poses no difficulty for us today.

3. To concede, on a variation of option 2, that the New Testament authors were not following the intention of the Old Testament authors, but to explain it as a function of apostolic authority. In other words, since they were inspired, they could do as they pleased. We are not inspired, so we cannot follow their lead.

In my opinion, all three of these views—although motivated by noble concerns to protect the Bible from abuse—will not stand up to close examination. As we go through the examples in this chapter, we will comment on these views here and there, but I will state my conclusions up front:

1. The New Testament authors were not engaging the Old Testament in an effort to remain consistent with the original context and intention of the Old Testament author.

2. They were indeed commenting on what the text *meant*.

3. The hermeneutical attitude they embodied should be embraced
and followed by the church today.

To put it succinctly, the New Testament authors were explaining what
the Old Testament means *in light of Christ's coming*.

It is important to understand that what we read in Luke 20 is just
one example not only of what we see so often in the pages of the New
Testament but of the manner in which other interpreters in the same
general time period use their Scripture. One of the main difficulties with
these three evangelical approaches is that they do not engage the New
Testament in the context of the hermeneutical world in which the New
Testament writers lived. Indeed, for some evangelicals, it seems necessary to create as much distance as possible between the New Testament
writers and the fanciful interpretations of their contemporaries.

Unfortunately, such a way of thinking creates many more problems
than it solves. The odd uses of the Old Testament by New Testament
authors are such a very common dimension of the New Testament that it
quickly becomes special pleading to argue otherwise. The incarnational
analogy outlined in this book suggests another way of approaching the
problem: *we must begin our understanding of **apostolic hermeneutics**
by first understanding, as best we can, the interpretive world in which the
New Testament was written*. Such an investigation will not tell the *whole*
story, but it is an absolutely vital component.

Moreover, locating apostolic hermeneutics in its historical setting does
not bring an end to the issue. In fact, it raises many thorny theological
issues of its own. For instance, if the misuse of the Old Testament by
contemporary pastors rubs us the wrong way, what right do we have to
reject it when a New Testament author does something similar? And if
we do accept the hermeneutical approach of the apostles as valid for
them, how should that affect how *we* use the Old Testament today?
These are perennial questions in the debate. In fact, it is precisely issues
such as these that incline evangelicals to try to find some other way
of explaining apostolic hermeneutics. These inclinations are perfectly
understandable, and at the end of this chapter I address them directly.
But before we do so, our first order of business is to understand—precisely because Christianity is a historical faith—the historical context
for apostolic hermeneutics.

Biblical Interpretation in the Second Temple Period

The historical setting in which the New Testament authors wrote
is often referred to as the **Second Temple period**, that is, the centu-

ries between the completion of the Second Temple in 516 BC and its destruction by the Romans in AD 70. It is also conventionally referred to as the intertestamental or postexilic period, but "Second Temple" is normally preferred.

In principle, awareness of a text's original setting is a common starting point for modern (including evangelical) scholarship, and for good reason. If one wishes to understand Galatians, one must understand something of the conflicts Paul had with the Judaizers. If one wishes to understand the differences between Chronicles and its parallels in Samuel–Kings, one must first have a broad understanding of some of the issues concerning postexilic Judaism. If one wishes to have greater clarity concerning the opening chapters of Genesis, one must have at least a broad sketch of the worldviews of the ancient Near East. To understand the Bible, historical context matters. Failure to interact with the historical context can lead to bizarre interpretations.

A convenient label often attached to such an approach is "grammatical-historical," meaning that the words of the text in front of you must be understood in their original grammatical (i.e., interpreting the text in the original language) and historical contexts. Although this is a healthy approach to reading literature in general, when this method is applied rigidly to apostolic hermeneutics, we sometimes find we have painted ourselves into a theological corner. We will look at this more below. But the important point here is this: the principle that "original context matters" must be applied not only to *grammar* and *history* but also to the **hermeneutics** of the New Testament writers. To understand how they handled the Old Testament, which reveals their hermeneutical standards, we must have a sketch of the hermeneutical world in which they lived. Again, as important as the original grammatical-historical context is for understanding ancient *texts*, so too is the original hermeneutical-historical context important for understanding ancient *hermeneutics*. With this in mind, below is a sketch of that ancient interpretive world. First we will look at the Old Testament itself and then at Second Temple literature.

Innerbiblical Interpretation: The Old Testament's Use of the Old Testament

The earliest examples of ancient biblical interpretation we have come from the Old Testament itself. As we glimpsed in the previous two chapters, the book of Chronicles as a whole is one such example. The author of this work, it seems fairly clear, is at least at times interacting specifically with texts in Samuel–Kings. At other times he is not interacting with these specific texts but referring more generally to certain episodes in Israel's past. Still, scholars recognize that numerous examples in Chronicles seem to be interacting with actual texts, one such example being the Passover law in 2 Chronicles 35:13 discussed in chapter 3.

Perhaps a better, and much celebrated, example is found in Daniel 9. There we read of Daniel's interpretation of the seventy years of Babylonian captivity prophesied by Jeremiah (Jer. 25:11; 29:10). There is some legitimate question as to what even Jeremiah meant by seventy, since Israel's stay in Babylon was really only about fifty years (the final deportation was in 587 BC and the Israelites returned in 538 BC). A number closer to seventy is found if one begins counting from the first wave of deportation in 605 BC. Or one could suggest that the seventy years of captivity represent the period between the destruction of the temple in 586 BC and the building of the Second Temple, which was completed in or around 516 BC (i.e., they weren't *really* back in the land until the temple had been completed).

However we might handle this issue, Daniel's view is very different. For him, the seventy years are to be understood in a surprising way, as "seventy sevens" of years. What is often stressed in certain evangelical circles concerning Daniel's interpretation is the matter of end-time prophecy. That is not at all my focus here. I am interested not in what "seventy sevens" means but in Daniel's handling of Jeremiah's prophecy this way.

As Daniel tells us, he "understood from the Scriptures, according to the word of the LORD given to Jeremiah the prophet, that the desolation of Jerusalem would last seventy years" (Dan. 9:2). He then prays to God for forgiveness for his people for their sins that brought them into exile. The key for us is 9:21–22:

> While I was still in prayer, Gabriel, the man I had seen in the earlier vision, came to me in swift flight about the time of the evening sacrifice. He instructed me and said to me, "Daniel, I have now come to give you insight and understanding."

Gabriel then proceeds to explain to him the *meaning* of Jeremiah's words: the seventy years really refer to "seventy sevens" of years. Daniel is able to arrive at this conclusion because Gabriel gives him "insight and understanding." It is by heavenly illumination that Daniel comes to understand the fuller, deeper measure of Jeremiah's prophecy. I think it is saying too much to suggest that Jeremiah's seventy years have *no* literal value (albeit as a round number). Still, the force of Daniel 9:21–22 should not be lost. Gabriel does not say, "Hey Daniel, here's a nice little twist I can give to Jeremiah's words so you can apply them to your situation." This is nothing less than illumination from heaven to provide Daniel with the deeper meaning contained in Jeremiah's words, meaning that Jeremiah himself neither intended nor could be expected on his own to understand.

We could look at other examples of innerbiblical interpretation. Whole books have been written on the subject (e.g., Michael Fishbane's *Biblical Interpretation in Ancient Israel*). But this one example in Daniel may be most relevant for us here. There are places where the Old Testament itself presents challenges to conventional, modern standards of interpretation. And we see something similar in the New Testament, where Old Testament passages are reunderstood by the New Testament authors to reflect a deeper reality than what was envisioned by the Old Testament authors.

Before we look at specific Second Temple examples, I would like to bring Jesus' words into the conversation. As the angel illumined Daniel with a deeper understanding of Scripture, we see Jesus doing something very similar at the end of Luke. In fact, I would say that he establishes a hermeneutical foundation for how the Old Testament is now to be understood by Christians:

> He said to them, "This is what I told you while I was still with you: Everything must be fulfilled that is written about me in the Law of Moses, the Prophets and the Psalms."
>
> Then he opened their minds so they could understand the Scriptures. He told them, "This is what is written: The Christ will suffer and rise from the dead on the third day, and repentance and forgiveness of sins will be preached in his name to all nations, beginning at Jerusalem. You are witnesses of these things." (Luke 24:44–48)

It is important to remember the context. Jesus has been raised from the dead and now appears to his disciples. And, as he did earlier with the two men on the road to Emmaus (Luke 24:13–35), Jesus instructs them about how to understand the Old Testament, or as Jesus puts it, "the Law of Moses, the Prophets and the Psalms," which is ancient shorthand for what we call the Old Testament. Clearly Jesus wants to impress upon the disciples that his death and resurrection and the spread of the gospel are the culmination of what the Scriptures say. But notice, in order to "understand the Scriptures," it was necessary for Jesus to "open their minds," to give them heavenly insight, as it were.

Also, notice what Jesus says is the *content* or *fulfillment* of the Old Testament when he says, "This is what is written": it is his death and resurrection and the subsequent spread of the gospel to all nations, beginning in Jerusalem. This raises many questions. Is that all there really is to the Old Testament? What about Job or Proverbs? Does Jesus' statement here account for every chapter of Exodus or Esther? Or perhaps is Jesus referring to several key Old Testament prophecies about himself?

Perhaps the most pressing question for us is where specifically does the Old Testament say that the Christ will suffer *and rise from the dead*. Some suggest Hosea 6:2 as a likely candidate:

> After two days he will revive us;
> on the third day he will restore us,
> that we may live in his presence.

But appealing to this one passage to find concrete textual support for Christ's resurrection borders on the absurd. Jesus is not saying that there are some interesting Old Testament prophecies that speak of him—flip through the Old Testament and see how many you can find. And if you are really clever you might even stumble onto Hosea 6:2 as a proof-text for the crucifixion and resurrection. Rather, he is saying that *all* Scriptures speak of him in the sense that he is *the climax of Israel's story*.

The Old Testament *as a whole* is about him, not a subliminal prophecy or a couple of lines tucked away in a minor prophet. Rather, Christ—who he is and what he did—is where the Old Testament has been leading all along. To see this requires that Christ open our minds as he did the minds of his disciples. In other words, to see how Christ fulfills the Old Testament—the whole story, not just some isolated prophecies—is not simply a matter of reading the Old Testament objectively, but reading it "Christianly," which is what we see in the New Testament time and time again.

But we are jumping ahead of ourselves a bit here. We have only glimpsed thus far the phenomenon of innerbiblical interpretation and the trajectories set within Scripture itself for how the text can be open to new, dynamic ways of understanding. The trajectories set within the pages of the Old Testament are seen not only in the pages of the New Testament but in Jewish interpretive texts of the Second Temple period. We will now look more closely at this period in an effort to gain further insight into the hermeneutical world of Christ and the apostles.

Biblical Interpretation in Second Temple Literature

The ancient world did not stand still in the centuries following Israel's return from exile. Much happened historically, including the passing of political control first from the Babylonians to the Persians, the Greeks (Alexander the Great), and the Romans. Each of these periods produced its own challenges to the Jewish people: matters of ethnic and religious identity and even pure survival. During this time Israel's literary activity is well documented.

The main bodies of extrabiblical literature that were written during this lengthy period include the Apocrypha, portions of the Pseudepigrapha, the Dead Sea Scrolls, and the works of **Philo** and **Josephus**. These represent a vast amount of literature. One could include the **Targums** (Aramaic translations of the Hebrew Old Testament) in this category. Although the final versions in existence today are of medieval origin, targumic activity is certainly pre-Christian, since Aramaic had by then already become the common language for Jews. (Furthermore, portions of Targums have been found among the Dead Sea Scrolls.)

At this juncture, we will look at only one example from the Apocrypha and one from the Dead Sea Scrolls. We could spend many more pages (books, in fact) unpacking other Second Temple texts, but studying even two examples will reveal a clear enough glimpse of the hermeneutical world in which the New Testament was written. More Second Temple texts will be brought up when we examine specific New Testament examples a bit later.

Apocrypha: Wisdom of Solomon

Apocrypha means "hidden things," a name that reflects that the books contained therein were not included in the Jewish canon. Eighteen books are normally considered part of this collection, but we will focus here on only one (fairly lengthy) example of biblical interpretation from the Wisdom of Solomon.

The Wisdom of Solomon is so called because a lot of it reads like biblical wisdom literature, mainly the first nine of its nineteen chapters. The author is anonymous but is conventionally referred to today as "Pseudo-Solomon" since he assumes a Solomonic persona (i.e., he takes on the character of Solomon). This simply represents a literary style of the time; it is not an act of deception. The book was written in Greek sometime between the latter part of the first century BC and early part of the first century AD, meaning that it was clearly not written by Solomon, who lived about eight hundred years before Greek became a vital language for Jews.

What is germane to our present discussion is that, by the time Pseudo-Solomon wrote his book, he was already heir to a long history of biblical interpretation in which certain interpretive conclusions had been reached. There are many interesting things to note, but we will limit our comments to chapter 10, where our author begins to tell the story of Israel's past. As the early portion of the book makes clear, his motive for doing so is to encourage his readers who are suffering under intense persecution by the Romans. He tells them Israel's story, beginning with

Adam (10:1) and culminating in the exodus (10:15–21), to show his readers how God has protected his people in the past and will continue to do so now. In this chapter Pseudo-Solomon lists a who's who of major Old Testament people (similar to Heb. 11) and devotes a few comments to each. What is important for us to see is that, for each person described, Pseudo-Solomon tells not simply an aspect of the *biblical story*, but an *interpretive tradition* about the biblical story that by his time had already become part of the common understanding of that biblical story.

I am not saying these traditions were universally held—far from it. In fact, there were various, even conflicting, interpretive traditions in existence in his day. My only point, as will become clear below, is that Pseudo-Solomon was heir to certain traditions, many of which are documented in other, earlier Second Temple texts. This is very important to understand. He was not the only one to say what he said, nor was he the first; his comments do not reflect his own private interpretive efforts. Rather, he is *one* witness among others that provides us today with a glimpse of how he and other Second Temple interpreters actually understood these biblical stories.

Another way of putting it is that Pseudo-Solomon had an "interpreted Bible" in his head, meaning he already had an interpretive grid available to him for how certain parts of the Bible were to be understood. And this grid was more or less simply assumed by him. Perhaps a modern illustration will help. In one of my classes I was challenging students to think of examples of where we have assumed that something is in the Bible when in fact it is not. One student answered, "Some people think that the names of the three wise men are found in the New Testament, but the fact of the matter is, we don't even know what the names of the three wise men were." This was a very interesting comment. True, some people assume that the names Caspar, Melchior, and Balthazar are found in the Gospels, although they are not. But neither are *three* wise men! The Gospels do not specify the number.

The point is that my student had a certain preunderstanding of what is and is not in the Bible, and that preunderstanding comes from how we were taught to understand the Bible—either through Sunday school, Christmas carols, television shows, or some other source. Moreover, this preunderstanding is largely unconscious. Apart from the absence of modern technology, the ancient world was not much different in this regard. They, too, had interpreted Bibles in their heads, evidence of which is plentiful in Second Temple literature.

With this in mind, we can now move to chapter 10 of the Wisdom of Solomon. In the following paragraphs, I cite a portion of this chapter, divided according to the biblical figure it refers to, and comment briefly on the part of the text that reflects the author's interpreted Bible (italic type). (Those wishing more detailed interaction with this passage, particularly with respect to parallel verses in other Second Temple literature, should consult the works listed at the end of this chapter, especially those by Kugel and Enns.) The recurring reference to wisdom where we might expect God should allow no distraction. The author is personifying wisdom, which reflects such passages as Proverbs 8, where wisdom is likewise personified as a woman. Note also that it is the author's style never to mention the biblical figures by name. Their identities, however, are not in question to anyone with even a general knowledge of the Old Testament.

Adam: "Wisdom protected the first-formed father of the world, when he alone had been created; *she delivered him from his transgression*, and gave him strength to rule all things" (Wis. 10:1–2). What is the transgression from which Adam was delivered? Does Genesis speak of any such thing? It is unclear where this bit of interpretation comes from, but one thing is certain: it meant something to Pseudo-Solomon, and we can assume it meant something to his hearers as well. It is their way of understanding the Adam story. It is worth noting that Pseudo-Solomon's interpretation does not intersect well with the Christian doctrine of original sin.

Cain: "But when an unrighteous man departed from her in his anger, he perished because in rage he killed his brother. *When the earth was flooded because of him*, wisdom again saved it, steering the righteous man by a paltry piece of wood" (Wis. 10:3–4). It seems here that Cain is the cause of the flood, something the Bible never says. The Bible, rather, attributes the cause of the flood to the wickedness of humankind, which seems to be connected to the strange interbreeding mentioned in Genesis 6:1–4 (the sons of God and daughters of men). Oddly, Pseudo-Solomon himself refers to the explanation given in Genesis 6 later on (Wis. 14:6), which might suggest just how unconscious his interpreted Bible is. The explanation for the flood he gives in Wisdom of Solomon 10:4 is not found in the Old Testament or, to the best of my knowledge, in any other Second Temple text. Does this mean that blaming Cain for the flood was Pseudo-Solomon's own invention? We must leave that option open. But that he can allude to it in such a shorthand manner suggests how deeply imbedded it was for him as well as for his readers.

Abraham: "Wisdom also, *when the nations in wicked agreement had been put to confusion*, recognized the righteous man and preserved him blameless before God, and kept him strong in the face of his compassion for his child" (Wis. 10:5). The "righteous man," Abraham, is closely connected here to another Old Testament story, the Tower of Babel, where "the nations in wicked agreement" (to build the tower) were "put to confusion." In fact, what this comment by Pseudo-Solomon implies is that Abraham was a *contemporary* of the tower episode. From the point of view of the strict chronology of Genesis, this is impossible. Still, this did not stop ancient interpreters from forging some connection between them. For one thing, the two stories appear side by side in Genesis, so seeking some connection would seem inviting.

Another Second Temple text (***Book of Biblical Antiquities***, first century AD) also places Abraham at the scene of the Tower of Babel. Specifically, Abraham refuses to take part in the building project. He is thrown into prison and threatened with death by fire in the brick ovens if he does not recant. God then comes to the rescue and delivers him from prison. Some versions of this tradition are also alluded to in many **rabbinic** texts. Ancient interpreters do not always lay out their logic for us, but the basis for this tradition may be what is for us a peculiar reading of Genesis 15:7: "I am the LORD, who brought you out of Ur of the Chaldeans." Ur is a city in Babylon (i.e., Chaldea), but it also looks like a Hebrew word for fire. So, ancient interpreters might have understood this verse not to be relaying a simple piece of geography but saying "I delivered you from the *fire* of Babylon." What fire is that? The fire of the ovens used to make the bricks for the Tower of Babel (Gen. 11:3).

Whatever the reason, the point once again is that Pseudo-Solomon was not the only ancient interpreter to forge this fairly intricate exegetical connection between Abraham and Babel. More precisely, we cannot say that it was Pseudo-Solomon himself who consciously forged this connection at all. This had already been done for him before he came on the scene. His comment is not evidence of his own interpretive activity, but of the extent to which such previous activity had become common knowledge.

Lot: "Wisdom rescued *a righteous man* when the ungodly were perishing; he escaped the fire that descended on the Five Cities" (Wis. 10:6). Was Lot really righteous? He was, at least according to Abraham's dialogue with his angelic visitors (Gen. 18:16–33). Abraham pleads with them not to destroy Sodom if any righteous people are found in the city. He begins, "What if there are fifty righteous people in the city?" (18:24) and works his way down to ten (18:32). The implication is that Lot and his family were the ones that Abraham was trying to save. But, to rephrase the question, how righteous was he, *really*? When he and his uncle Abraham were parting ways (Gen. 13), Abraham gave him first choice of where to go, and he decided, of all places, to pitch his tents "*near* Sodom" (13:12). This is a remarkable choice given that the very next verse tells us how wicked that place was. Then in 19:3, it is clear that Lot no longer lives near Sodom but *inside* the city, in a *house*. In fact, according to 19:1, he was "sitting in the gateway of the city" when the angelic party arrived, an indication that he had some governmental authority (judges settled disputes at the city gates).

Some Second Temple interpreters understood these clues in the text to indicate that Lot was quite comfortable in Sodom and so gave him a negative assessment. For example, in addition to Pseudo-Solomon, other interpreters made the point that Lot was delivered from Sodom by virtue of *Abraham's* merit, not his own (e.g., Philo, *Targum Pseudo-Jonathan*). For Pseudo-Solomon to assign Lot to the category "righteous," although certainly justifiable biblically (and this is picked up in 2 Pet. 2:7), is nevertheless to come down on one side of an interpretive issue for which two sides exist.

Jacob: "She protected him from his enemies, and kept him safe from *those who lay in wait for him*; in his arduous contest she gave him the victory, so that he might learn that godliness is more powerful than anything else" (Wis. 10:12). As the preceding verses make clear (10:10–11), the subject here is Jacob. But there is no mention in Genesis of anyone lying in wait for Jacob. Perhaps one might think of some episode with Esau, but Genesis is very clear. In Genesis 33, when Jacob sees Esau and his army advancing, Jacob panics and sends messengers before him, thinking he would need to appease Esau. When they finally meet, Esau is actually overjoyed to see his younger brother, despite the trickery of Jacob to secure his older brother's birthright (Gen. 27). Why, then, does Pseudo-Solomon say what the Bible not only does not say but flatly contradicts?

One begins to answer that question by observing once again that Pseudo-Solomon is not the only ancient interpreter to tell a similar story. In fact, one early Second Temple text, **Jubilees** (second century BC), tells how Esau and his men laid an ambush for Jacob. A battle ensued and Esau was killed. Hence, we have in the Wisdom of Solomon another allusion, however brief, to a preexisting interpretive tradition. However out of accord with the Bible it might seem to us, our task here is not to pass judgment on Second Temple interpreters but to understand them. That Pseudo-Solomon can refer to it so briefly speaks to how widely recognizable and accepted this tradition must have been.

Joseph: "And when he was in prison she did not leave him, until she brought him the scepter of a kingdom and authority over his masters. *Those who accused him* she showed to be false, and she gave him everlasting honor" (Wis. 10:14). Who were Joseph's accusers (plural)? Not his brothers. They do not accuse him of anything. They just throw him into a well and sell him into slavery. Moreover, his being sold into slavery is dealt with earlier in 10:13. Here in 10:14 the topic is clearly his being accused by Potiphar's wife of making advances on her. But she is only one—why does Pseudo-Solomon speak of multiple accusers? It may be that Genesis 39:14 provides an explanation. Potiphar's wife, addressing her household servants, says, "Look . . . this Hebrew has been brought to *us* to make sport of *us*!" Has Joseph's alleged advances on Potiphar's wife really made sport of *all* of them? It is curious, too, that in 39:17, just three verses later, Potiphar's wife, speaking to her husband, accuses Joseph of making "sport of *me*." One explanation for the tradition of multiple accusers is that early interpreters capitalized on this grammatical irritant by inventing a story of multiple accusers to account for 39:14. Such careful attention to minor details in the text (in Hebrew the difference between "of us" and "of me" is just a matter of a small suffix) is typical of Second Temple interpretation.

But the ultimate biblical motivation for this interpretation is not the focus here. More to the point is that this same interpretive tradition is found in another ancient text, *Life of Joseph*, written by Philo (roughly contemporary with Pseudo-Solomon). He puts into the mouth of Potiphar's wife the accusation that Joseph not only made advances on her but had a track record of doing the same with her maidens. It is such accusers that Pseudo-Solomon says wisdom "showed to be false." Once again, Pseudo-Solomon's comments participate in a Second Temple interpretive tradition that, however disconnected from the Bible it may appear to us, required no explanation then.

The remainder of our examples from the Wisdom of Solomon concern Pseudo-Solomon's interpretation of the exodus (10:15–21). We will look at three examples from 10:18–21, all pertaining to the crossing of the Red Sea:

> She brought them over the Red Sea,
> and led them through deep waters;
> but she drowned their enemies,
> and *cast them up from the depth of the sea.*
> *Therefore the righteous plundered the ungodly;*
> they sang hymns, O Lord, to your holy name,
> and praised with one accord your defending hand;
> for wisdom opened the mouths of those who were mute,
> and *made the tongues of infants speak clearly.*

Casting up soldiers: That wisdom is said to "cast" the Egyptian soldiers "up from the depth of the sea" reflects an ancient interpretive tradition that is found in its most complete form in *Targum Pseudo-Jonathan* and some later rabbinic texts. The motive for this tradition seems to be a reading of Exodus 14–15 that attempts to account for some curious details. In Exodus 14:30 we read that the Egyptians are seen dead, washed up on the *shore*. In 15:5, however, we read that they sank like a stone in the *sea*. Then in 15:12, they are said to be swallowed by the *earth*. To us the biblical logic seems straightforward: the Egyptian army drowns in the sea (thus sinking; 15:5), and then, as one would fully expect, the bodies are washed up onto the shore in plain view of all (14:30). The expression in 15:12 "the earth swallowed them" is simply an ancient idiom meaning "they died."

Targum Pseudo-Jonathan contains another, rather fanciful, way of addressing these biblical verses, however. The sea and earth had an argument about who would bear the responsibility for accepting the Egyptian dead. Both thought God would be angry with them, so each refused. Only when God intervened and assured the land that he would not be angry with it for accepting the Egyptian dead was the problem solved: the sea *cast* the heretofore sunken/drowned soldiers onto the shore and the earth swallowed them. Thus, a story was created to account for all three verses in Exodus. Even though the targumic and rabbinic versions of this interpretive tradition are later than the Wisdom of Solomon, Pseudo-Solomon is clearly participating in some early version of that tradition. Or, to put it a better way, the Wisdom of Solomon bears witness to how old this tradition really is. For Pseudo-Solomon to be able to allude to this tradition in such an abbreviated manner indicates how well traveled this tradition already was by his time.

Plundering the soldiers: Another allusion to an interpretive tradition is the mention of the Israelites "plundering" the dead soldiers on the shore. The Egyptians being cast up onto the shore is what allowed the Israelites to do so (note the use of "therefore"). The question again is, if the Bible does not say this, why would Pseudo-Solomon? One possible reason for inserting this piece of information is to explain a nagging detail later in the story. In Exodus 17, the Israelites find themselves at war with the Amalekites. One might well ask where the Israelites got their weapons from. Any answer to this question is conjectural, but one answer given by early interpreters is that they stripped the dead Egyptian soldiers of their weapons. This tradition is explicitly attested in Josephus's *Jewish Antiquities* 2.16.6 §349 (late first century AD). Early interpreters might have gone looking for a convenient place in the biblical narrative to insert such a needed explanation. Exodus 14:30, "Israel saw the Egyptians lying dead on the shore," provided such an insertion point. And, as with the other interpretive traditions we have seen thus far, Pseudo-Solomon is not alone in this among ancient interpreters.

Out of the mouths of babes: Finally, Pseudo-Solomon says that infants also sang at the sea. The song he is referring to is Exodus 15:1–18, called the "Song at the Sea" or the "Song of Moses and Miriam." But infants are not said to sing in the biblical account. This tradition is found, however, in *Targum Pseudo-Jonathan* and picked up by many important rabbinic sources. Why this tradition arose in the first place is not at all clear. What is clear is that many ancient interpretive sources include this tradition in their retelling of Exodus 15. The Wisdom of Solomon shows that this tradition had found its way into common circulation by at least the early part of the first century AD. And so, this and the other traditions glimpsed here provide a window to how some ancient interpreters understood their Bibles.

Even though we have been focusing on only one chapter in the Wisdom of Solomon, other Second Temple texts have been brought into the discussion. This is inevitable. Any interpretive tradition in one Second Temple text necessarily brings you into contact with many other ancient interpreters who incorporate that same (or similar) tradition. In other words, to understand the Wisdom of Solomon, we have had to go beyond it, to the hermeneutical environment of which it is a part. And ancient retellings of the Bible, such as we find here, include ways of understanding those stories that are the fruit of ancient interpretive activity and that made their way into common circulation, so much so that Pseudo-Solomon could refer to them in such an abbreviated fashion.

What is true for the Wisdom of Solomon is true for the New Testament: to understand the way in which the New Testament authors handle the Old Testament requires that we understand their hermeneutical context. Later in this chapter we will see similarities between the New Testament's use of the Old Testament and that of other Second Temple texts, both in terms of the interpretive *methods* used and the interpretive *traditions* adopted. Keeping both methods and traditions in view is vitally important.

Dead Sea Scrolls: 1QpHab

The Dead Sea Scrolls, the first of which were discovered accidentally in a Judean cave in 1947 (near the town of Qumran, hence the alternate name "**Qumran scrolls**"), are the most important manuscript finds pertaining to biblical studies in the modern world. They have shed much light on many issues, the most important of which for us concerns biblical interpretation. In this respect, they are most accommodating. What we have in the Dead Sea Scrolls are actual commentaries, perhaps not in the sense that we are familiar with, but commentaries nonetheless. The typical practice was to cite a brief portion of a biblical book, followed by its interpretation. The Hebrew word for interpretation is *pesher*, which is why these texts are referred to as pesher commentaries.

We will look at one example from a text known as **1QpHab** (meaning cave 1, Qumran, pesher on Habakkuk). Specifically, we will look at how this text handles Habakkuk 1:5. In the context of Habakkuk, God is promising to answer Habakkuk's cry to punish those who do injustice. And God's remedy truly does "amaze" Habakkuk: God promises to send in the Babylonians, Israel's hated enemy, to punish God's people (1:6). This is not at all the solution that Habakkuk was hoping for.

For the Qumran interpreters, however, there was a hidden meaning to these words. They interpreted this prophecy in a way that had absolutely nothing whatsoever to do with its function in the book of Habakkuk. This is because Qumran interpretation rested on two related assumptions. First, they believed that true biblical interpretation can be only what is divinely revealed (similar to what we saw in Dan. 9, for example), that is, by divine illumination. Second, the Bible has its ultimate and final meaning in the events surrounding the Qumran community. Whatever the text meant back then is not what the text *really* means. Rather, according to the Qumran community, the prophets' words *really* refer to the events of the day, because the community considered themselves to be living in the time of the true fulfillment of the biblical story. To put it another way, they considered themselves to be living in the end time, the **eschaton**. And this eschatological meaning of the ancient prophecy was not known to the prophet or to anyone else other than those to whom the "Teacher of Righteousness" (mentioned below and likely referring to the founder of the Qumran sect) revealed it.

Already here we should take note of some similarities with what we have seen in Luke 24. Jesus reveals to his disciples the understanding of what the Old Testament is *really* about—Christ. This is not to say that the Dead Sea Scrolls and the New Testament are made of the same material, but they are certainly recognizable to each other. Perhaps we can see this more clearly by looking at how 1QpHab interprets Habakkuk 1:5. The biblical passage is as follows:

> Look at the nations and watch—
>   and be utterly amazed.
> For I am going to do something in your days
>   that you would not believe,
>   even if you were told.

The commentary begins:

> [Interpreted, this concerns] those who were unfaithful together with the Liar, in that they [did] not [listen to the word received by] the Teacher of Righteousness from the mouth of God. (ii 1–3)

This interpretation (*pesher*) may be derived from a very sophisticated handling of certain Hebrew words in Habakkuk: "unfaithful" (*bo-ge-dim*) in 1QpHab may be a play on the Hebrew phrase *at the nations* in Habakkuk 1:5, which looks similar (*bag-goy-im*). Now, objectively, this would simply be wrong. More importantly, and what complicates the matter, is that the Septuagint (Greek) version of Habakkuk 1:5 *does* have a word that approximates "unfaithful," thus suggesting that the Hebrew text from which the Greek was translated differs from what we have in our Hebrew Old Testaments today. This raises the complex issue of what the Old Testament looked like that the Qumran community had access to or, more to the point, whether there even was a fixed Old Testament text at that time, since the Dead Sea Scrolls contain multiple Hebrew versions of the Old Testament. Either way, these early interpreters reveled in such challenges to anchor what they *knew* to be right about a biblical text, either by manipulating the text or following other versions that suited their purposes.

But let's not lose sight of the big picture. What in Habakkuk 1:5 referred to God's promise to bring the Babylonians to punish Israel is now turned into a condemnation of the enemies of the Qumran community. (The "Liar" may refer to the main adversary of the Teacher of Righteousness.) So, according to this Qumran interpreter, Habakkuk is *really* talking about the troubles surrounding the founding of the Qumran sect. But there is more:

> And it concerns the unfaithful of the New [Covenant] in that they have not believed in the Covenant of God [and have profaned] His holy Name. (ii 3–4)

Habakkuk 1:5 does not have just one meaning, but a second: those who were among the "New Covenant" but have profaned God's name (by resisting the sect). In other words, if the first interpretation has in view resistance at the sect's *founding*, the *backsliding* of those who had made an original commitment is in view here.

The Qumran community finds yet a third interpretation to this one verse:

> And likewise, this saying is to be interpreted [as concerning those who] will be unfaithful at the end of the days. They, the men of violence and the breakers of the Covenant, will not believe when they hear all that [is to happen to] the final generation from the Priest [in whose heart] God set [understanding] that he might interpret all the words of His servants the Prophets, through whom He foretold all that would happen to His people and [His land]. (ii 5–10)

Here the focus is not on the past or present, but the future: "those who *will be* unfaithful at the end of the days."

Three meanings for one passage, and not one of them in the least concerned with whether it adheres to the meaning intended in the book of Habakkuk. It is safe to say that the interpretation of Habakkuk 1:5 in 1QpHab is not an exercise in grammatical-historical exegesis. It is quite plainly an exercise in reading into the prophet's words what the interpreter already knew those words were really about (as the last portion of the third comment makes clear). For the Qumran community, biblical interpretation was not a means of discovering ancient meaning but of using the Bible to validate the present self-understanding of the Qumran community.

What Can We Learn from Second Temple Literature?

It may seem that these examples have been drawn out further than they need to be. But in reality, we have barely scratched the surface. Much of the phenomenon of Second Temple biblical interpretation can be fully understood only by working with the original languages, something we have been able to only touch upon ("Ur/fire" connecting Abraham with Babel in the Wisdom of Solomon; possibly the play on the words *unfaithful* and *nations* in 1QpHab). Still, we can see in the Dead Seas Scrolls that these early interpreters seemed to anchor their interpretations in what they *knew* to be right. This involved manipulating the text to suit their purposes. And even though the Qumran community had a particular sectarian impulse to it (e.g., their relentless focus on their community as being the focus of prophetic fulfillment) and its interpretive *conclusions* may have differed significantly from those of other Jewish communities of the time, their interpretive *methods* are firmly at home in the Second Temple period.

Even this brief look at texts of this period begins to reveal a picture that would become much clearer if space allowed further examples. (Those interested can refer to some of the works listed at the end of the chapter.) Still, we have a broad but accurate sketch of Second Temple interpretation in both the exegetical *techniques* they employed and the interpretive *traditions* they adopted. These biblical interpreters exhibit for us an attitude toward biblical interpretation that operates on very different standards from those of modern interpreters. They were not motivated to reproduce the intention of the original human author. They were much more concerned to dig beneath the surface to reveal things ("mysteries" as the Qumran scrolls put it) that the untrained and impatient reader would miss.

With this said, we can now turn to the New Testament, which is also a Second Temple interpretive text. This is not to say that it reflects precisely the examples above. Nevertheless, we should expect the New Testament, being a Second Temple phenomenon, to behave in a way that would make it recognizable to its contemporaries, rather than expecting it to conform to our own twenty-first-century expectations.

Apostolic Hermeneutics as a Second Temple Phenomenon: Interpretive Methods

We have already looked at one example of the use of interpretive methods in the New Testament that seem odd to us but were right at home in the Second Temple world. Jesus' use of Exodus 3:6 in Luke 20:34–38, to say the least, is not an example of grammatical-historical exegesis. Evangelicals tend to protect Jesus and the apostles from the charge of engaging in such uncontrolled exegesis. It is argued that the New Testament authors employ the Old Testament for apologetic purposes. Hence, the logic goes, we can safely say that Jesus and the New Testament authors would *never* have done such wild things with the Old Testament if their purpose was to convince others of the gospel. This logic is completely misguided. We must remember how the teachers of the law reacted to Jesus' exegesis of Exodus 3:6: they were highly impressed (Luke 20:39–40). It is precisely *because* Jesus employed Second Temple techniques that his interpretation was *able* to have apologetic import.

Furthermore, it will not do to argue that Jesus and the apostles adopted such tainted exegetical techniques simply as an accommodation to the faulty thinking of their contemporaries. There simply is no indication of this anywhere in the New Testament. In fact, Paul's letters were not written to convince unbelieving Jews but to the churches, to those who needed no such apologetic thrust. To argue in such a way reveals more about our own assumptions concerning the supposed universal validity of our own hermeneutical standards than it does about apostolic hermeneutics. But apostolic hermeneutics is not to be explained in such a way as to conform to our expectations, nor should we be embarrassed about it or make excuses for it. It is to be understood. Toward that end, below are a few more examples of New Testament authors employing ancient interpretive methods.

Matthew 2:15 and Hosea 11:1

It is widely recognized that Matthew's Gospel is geared toward a Jewish audience. Hence, Matthew brings the Old Testament into his Gospel more times than the other three Gospels. He also does so in a way that seems strained to modern eyes. One such example is Matthew's use of Hosea 11:1:

And having been warned in a dream not to go back to Herod, they returned to their country by another route.

When they had gone, an angel of the Lord appeared to Joseph in a dream. "Get up," he said, "take the child and his mother and escape to Egypt. Stay there until I tell you, for Herod is going to search for the child to kill him."

So he got up, took the child and his mother during the night and left for Egypt, where he stayed until the death of Herod. *And so was fulfilled what the Lord had said through the prophet: "Out of Egypt I called my son."* (Matt. 2:12–15)

For Matthew, Jesus' trip as a boy to Egypt to escape Herod is a fulfillment of Hosea 11:1. Strictly speaking, Hosea's words are not fulfilled with Jesus going down *to* Egypt, but only upon his return. By citing Hosea 11:1, Matthew clearly anticipates that Jesus would eventually come out of Egypt, which is more in line with the wording of Hosea.

But the real problem is this: scanning the context of Hosea 11, it becomes quite clear that Hosea himself is not talking about the boy Jesus, nor is he thinking of a future messiah. In fact, Hosea 11 is not looking to the future at all but simply alluding to the past, as the context of 11:1 makes clear:

> When Israel was a child, I loved him,
>   and *out of Egypt I called my son.*
> But the more I called Israel,
>   the further they went from me.
> They sacrificed to the Baals
>   and they burned incense to images.
> It was I who taught Ephraim to walk,
>   taking them by the arms;
> but they did not realize
>   it was I who healed them. (Hos. 11:1–3)

Hosea's point here is that Israel is God's child, his son, and he loved him. And so he delivered Israel from Egypt. But, in return, the Israelites turned to idolatry. This passage is not predictive of Christ's coming but retrospective of Israel's disobedience.

It would take a tremendous amount of mental energy to argue that Matthew is respecting the historical context of Hosea's words, that is, that there actually is something predictive in Hosea 11. In the end such arguments serve only to support one's assumptions rather than challenge them. What motivates Matthew to handle Hosea's words as he does is not a desire to do grammatical-historical exegesis. Rather, I see a twofold motivation. First, in writing to a Jewish audience, such a handling of the Old Testament would not have seemed strange but very familiar. Once again, foremost in our minds must be how this use of the Old Testament would have been heard at *that* time, not in our time. Of course, Jews not believing in Christ would have disagreed with Matthew, but *not* because their exegetical sensibilities would have been violated. They would have disagreed because they did not share Matthew's faith in Christ.

This leads to the second point. Matthew was motivated by his conviction that Christ is the focus of Scripture, much like what we saw above with respect to Luke 24. It is because Matthew *knew* that Jesus was the Christ that he also knew that all Scripture speaks of him. But to say this is not to suggest a superficial rummaging through the Old Testament in search of proof-texts. Rather Matthew's use of Hosea reflects broader theological convictions. Although neither I nor anyone else can step into Matthew's head and outline precisely how he understood Hosea, the following suggestion is quite reasonable. It may be that Matthew had in mind not simply this one verse in Hosea 11, but the larger context of that chapter. There were no verse numbers in Matthew's day. Quoting one verse may have been a way of saying "that part of Hosea that begins with 'out of Egypt I called my son.'"

If this is true (and although this is not merely a private opinion, it is conjectural nonetheless), we may be able to trace some of Matthew's broader theological underpinnings. The son in Hosea and the son in Matthew are a study in contrasts. Israel came out of Egypt, was disobedient, deserved punishment, yet was forgiven by God (Hos. 11:8–11). Christ came out of Egypt, led a life of perfect obedience, deserved no punishment, but was crucified—the guiltless for the guilty. By presenting Jesus this way, Matthew was able to mount an argument for his readers that Jesus fulfilled the ideal that Israel was supposed to have reached but never did. Jesus is the true Israel.

Again, this is just one way of putting together Matthew's theological logic, and it is certainly up for debate. What is certain, however, is that Matthew's use of Hosea most definitely had an internal logic that was meaningful to his readers. Our obligation is to try to understand Matthew as he would have been understood by his original audience, not as we would like to understand him. I should make one final observation. Matthew does not say that the events in Jesus' boyhood life fulfill *Hosea's* words. He says that they fulfill what "the *Lord* had said through the prophet." It is what God says that is important, and what God said is not captured by the surface meaning of the words on the page, but by looking at the grander scope of God's overall redemptive plan.

2 Corinthians 6:2 and Isaiah 49:8

Toward the end of 2 Corinthians 5, Paul reminds his readers that they are God's ambassadors (5:20), meaning that God is making his appeal through them. Since, therefore, they are in such an exalted position, they must be careful not to "receive God's grace in vain" (6:1). In support of this, Paul cites Isaiah 49:8:

> As God's fellow workers we urge you not to receive God's grace in vain. For he says,
>
>> "In the time of my favor I heard you,
>>   and in the day of salvation I helped you."
>
> I tell you, now is the time of God's favor, now is the day of salvation.
> (2 Cor. 6:1–2)

As with Matthew, Paul attributes these words to God and not to Isaiah ("for he [God] says"). This should already cause us to anticipate that we will have to reorient our expectations for how these words function in their new context. If we look at the original context of Isaiah's prophecy, we see that what is in view is the future deliverance of Israel from Babylon, which is the topic of much of Isaiah, beginning in chapter 40. Isaiah 49:8 speaks of Israel's eventual restoration. There is nothing here at all about being reconciled to God in Christ, as Paul uses these words.

So, what is Paul doing here? I have heard 2 Corinthians 6:2 used in evangelistic services. "*Now* is the time of salvation," meaning, "Accept Christ now, today. You may die tonight." However true this may be, it is not at all what Paul is talking about here. The "now" of which Paul speaks is not our *individual* "now" but an **eschatological** "now." What drove Paul to handle Isaiah's words this way is his fundamental conviction that with the coming of Christ, the last days, the fullness of time, is upon us (e.g., see Gal. 4:4). Paul does not mean "accept Christ as your personal savior." He is, after all, speaking to *Christians* at Corinth. He means that the future deliverance spoken of by Isaiah regarding Israel and Babylon was prelude to a much larger event of deliverance, the coming of Christ and the deliverance of people from sin. The "day" that Isaiah spoke of began at Christ's resurrection and has been in effect for two thousand years. The deliverance looked forward to by Isaiah has happened for Paul *in Christ*, a fact indicated by Paul's changing the future tense of Isaiah 49:8 to the past tense.

As is typical of apostolic hermeneutics in general, Paul's intention in appealing to Isaiah 49:8 was not to do a bit of modern, scientific exegesis. It was, rather, an interpretive exercise founded on his conviction that Christ is the ultimate fulfillment of Israel's story. What God did for the Israelites back then in delivering them from Babylon and reestablishing them in the land, however real and historical it certainly was, for Paul must now be seen in a much larger and climactic context. Isaiah's words do not predict Christ, but now that Christ has come, Isaiah's words must be understood not on their own terms but as a preliminary phase of God's redemptive plan. Christ does not "fulfill" Isaiah 49:8 in the sense of a simple, so-called predictive prophecy. Rather, the redemptive work of God, which for Isaiah is focused on one people rescued from a foreign country at one moment in history, is seen by Paul as being "superfulfilled" in God's final, once-for-all, redemptive act for all of humanity.

Galatians 3:16, 29 and Abraham's "Seed"

In Galatians 3 Paul employs an exegetical technique that is well documented in both Second Temple texts and later rabbinic works. Again, if we begin our investigation with the conviction that Paul, a first-century Jew who was trained as a Pharisee (Phil. 3:4–6), should fit in his contemporary hermeneutical surroundings, perhaps we can look at Paul's words here without modern prejudice.

In Galatians 3:15–29, Paul argues that one is truly Abraham's heir by promise, not by adherence to the law. This is because the promises spoken to Abraham were made 430 years before the law was even put into effect (see 3:17). Hence, those who are truly Abraham's heirs are those who likewise are children of promise, not of law. Much here has occupied New Testament scholars, but we will focus on only one issue: Paul's grammatical argument based on the word *seed*:

> The promises were spoken to Abraham and to his seed. The Scripture does not say "and to seeds," meaning many people, but "and to your seed," meaning one person, who is Christ.

It is not exactly clear what Old Testament passage Paul is referring to here. Paul simply says "the Scripture." He likely has in view, however, such passages as Genesis 12:7, 13:15, and 24:7:

> The LORD said to Abram after Lot had parted from him, "Lift up your eyes from where you are and look north and south, east and west. All the land that you see I will give to you and your offspring forever. I will make your offspring like the dust of the earth, so that if anyone could count the dust, then your offspring could be counted. Go, walk through the length and breadth of the land, for I am giving it to you." (Gen. 13:14–17)

God's promise of land to Abraham was not only for him, but for his "offspring," which is the New International Version's translation of the Hebrew word for seed, *zera* (Greek *sperma*). *Zera* is a collective noun; that is, it is singular in *form* but both singular and plural in *meaning*, just like the English word *seed*. What is abundantly clear in the Genesis passages listed above, however, is that "seed" (translated "offspring") is plural. The promise that God made to Abraham is very specific. It concerns the *land* that will be given to Abraham's offspring, his seed, his descendants, which will number more than the stars in the sky or sand on the beach (Gen. 13:16 [cited above]; 15:5; 22:17).

But Paul interprets this biblical episode to refer not to the promise of land to numerous descendants but to the means by which one is reconciled to God: it is through promise, not law. And he anchors his interpretation to the singular form of the word. Paul here is employing a technique that was common in his day, namely, capitalizing on the interpretive flexibility of certain words or grammatical features. Such an explanation can cause problems for some evangelicals: Paul is using the Old Testament in a way that has nothing to do with how the Old Testament is to be understood in its original context. The theological point that Paul is arguing here is one that any Christian should say "amen" to, but how Paul got there can be troubling.

An added piece of information is found in Galatians 3:29. There Paul caps his argument that *all* come to be sons of God (3:26) through Christ. What had been causes for division (i.e., being Jew or Greek, slave or free, male or female) now count for nothing. Being Abraham's offspring is now determined by whether you belong to Christ:

> You are all sons of God through faith in Christ Jesus, for all of you who were baptized into Christ have clothed yourselves with Christ. There is neither Jew nor Greek, slave nor free, male nor female, for you are all one in Christ Jesus. *If you belong to Christ, then you are Abraham's seed*, and heirs according to the promise. (Gal. 3:26–29, italics added)

The way the church appropriates the promise to Abraham (reinterpreted as it is by Paul) is through *union* with Christ. In Galatians 3:29 Paul says that *belonging* to Christ makes you Abraham's seed. Furthermore, in referring to Christians in 3:29, Paul understands "seed" in the collective sense: "If *you* [*hymeis*, plural] belong to Christ, then *you are* [*este*, plural] Abraham's seed." The point that Paul seems to be making here is a deeply theological one. It is certainly not the case that he did not know that "seed" is a collective noun. That would be a ridiculous argument to make, that Paul did not know his Hebrew. Also, his collective use of "seed" in 3:29 demonstrates that he knew what he was doing. Rather, Paul seizes the grammatical ambiguity of the word, in good Second Temple fashion, and uses it to make a profound point about Christ and his people. Christ alone is truly Abraham's seed, the one who embodies Israel's ideal. The church is also Abraham's seed (collective), but only insofar as we "belong to Christ," *the* seed (singular). The church is Abraham's offspring, but only because Christ was Abraham's offspring first.

Paul did not derive this notion from reading his Old Testament objectively. Rather, he began with his conviction that Christ is the focus of the New Testament and then read Old Testament seed theology in light of that fact. For Paul, whatever meaning the Old Testament had in this regard now has a deeper meaning in light of Christ's coming. It is beyond question whether Paul's hermeneutic here should take its place among other Second Temple interpreters. A better question is how evangelicals can articulate a meaningful notion of apostolic authority in light of this type of exegetical behavior, which more or less boils down to the question "Can or should Paul's methods be reproduced today?" We will look at this later in this chapter, after we look at several more examples.

Romans 11:26–27 and Isaiah 59:20

Toward the end of what is a very difficult section in Romans (chapters 9–11), Paul starts to wind down his argument. What is often the focus of attention is Paul's conviction that *"all* Israel will be saved" (11:26). Our interest here is Paul's use of Isaiah 59:20. Actually, his citation includes Isaiah 59:21 and a portion of Jeremiah 31:33–34, but we are interested here only in the first part of the quotation:

> And so all Israel will be saved, as it is written:
>> "*The deliverer will come from Zion*;
>>> he will turn godlessness away from Jacob.
>> And this is my covenant with them
>>> when I take away their sins."

Paul says that the deliverer, by which he means Christ, will come *from Zion*. The citation in Isaiah looks like this:

> From the west, men will fear the name of the LORD,
>> and from the rising of the sun, they will revere his glory.
> For he will come like a pent-up flood
>> that the breath of the LORD drives along.
> "*The Redeemer will come to Zion*,
>> to those in Jacob who repent of their sins,"
> declares the LORD.

First of all, for Isaiah, the Redeemer (the same as "deliverer" in Paul) seems to be God himself: *"He* will come" in the previous line refers to the Lord, mentioned at the beginning. So, Paul applies to Christ what originally referred to God. Of course, no Christian will have a problem with this. It is a wonderful (if only a bit hidden) example of the New Testament's attitude toward the divinity of Christ. But the larger point should not be lost: God's redemption of Israel from exile (Isaiah) is now a picture of Christ's redemption of Israel from sin (Paul). Deliverance from Babylon pointed to a much bigger realization of *true* deliverance/redemption for Israel, which can be found only in Christ.

But we must note that Paul adjusts the wording of Isaiah to reflect his theological goal. The Hebrew version of Isaiah 59:21 has the redeemer coming *to* Zion (the preposition *lamed*). The Septuagint is similar in that it uses the preposition *heneken* ("for the sake of"). The point is that the original Old Testament sense is that God will come *to* Zion, or *for the sake of* Zion, to deliver it from exile. Zion here represents the people of Israel (elsewhere in the Old Testament it refers to Jerusalem). For Paul, however, the deliverer is not one who will come *to* Zion to deliver *it*. He will come *from* Zion. Zion describes not those to be delivered but Christ's point of origin. What precisely Paul means is unclear. Perhaps he is referring to Christ's coming from among his own people—he is a Jew. Or it could refer to Zion understood as a heavenly Jerusalem. However this is solved, which is of no consequence here, I wish only to point out that Paul's use of the Old Testament includes changing the preposition *to* (or *for the sake of* if he had the Septuagint in mind) to *from*.

One could suggest, perhaps, that Paul is not actually changing the Old Testament but that his reading of Isaiah 59:20 bears witness to another form of this passage that existed in his day. This may protect Paul against the accusation that he is running roughshod over the Old Testament, but it certainly raises a much larger problem: Paul's Old Testament actually looked different from ours. Solving one evangelical problem would raise another. Moreover, there is no evidence for any such alternate form of Isaiah 59:20. What we do have plenty of evidence for, however, is the interpretive practices of Second Temple interpreters, and it is there that we must try to understand Paul's use of Isaiah 59:20 in Romans 11:26. Paul's interpretive practices were firmly at home in his world.

Hebrews 3:7–11 and Psalm 95:9–10

The last example of interpretive methods we will look at is the use of Psalm 95:9–10 by the anonymous author of Hebrews. Here we have a situation similar to what we see in Romans 11:26: an Old Testament passage is changed, this time by adding one small word. And as we saw in Galatians 3, the purpose for this interpretive move was to support a fundamental theological conviction.

Much of the book of Hebrews argues that Christ is better than the means of revelation found in the Old Testament. That contrast is made explicit in 1:1–2. The author continues by contrasting Jesus to angels (1:4–2:18). Next Hebrews portrays Jesus as the new and better Moses (3:1–4:13). The contrast is introduced in 3:1–6 and carried further in 3:7–11, where the author quotes Psalm 95:7–11:

> Today, if you hear his voice,
> do not harden your hearts as you did at Meribah,
> as you did that day at Massah in the desert,
> *where your fathers tested and tried me,*
> *though they had seen what I did.*
> *For forty years I was angry with that generation;*
> I said, "They are a people whose hearts go astray,
> and they have not known my ways."
> So I declared on oath in my anger,
> "They shall never enter my rest."

The portion important for our discussion is in italic type. With only minor differences overall, both the Hebrew and Septuagint of Psalm 95 reflect the New International Version translation given above: the Israelites tested God in the desert, even though they had seen his miracles (i.e., exodus, water, and manna), and as a result God was angry with that generation. God's anger was demonstrated in the forty years of wilderness wandering for the Israelites. The rebellious generation died off before the others were allowed to enter their "rest" (95:11).

The citation of the psalm in Hebrews differs in many details, some of which are more important than others. The main issue for us is the insertion of the Greek word *dio* ("therefore") in 3:10. Greek grammar requires this small word to be first in a sentence. Hence, its insertion here makes a sentence break at a very crucial juncture. Whereas Psalm 95 equates forty years with the *period of God's wrath*, Hebrews, by inserting *dio*, equates the forty years with the *duration of God's works*. Here is Hebrews 3:7–11:

> So, as the Holy Spirit says:
> "Today, if you hear his voice,
> do not harden your hearts
> as you did in the rebellion,
> during the time of testing in the desert,

> *where your fathers tested and tried me*
> *and for <u>forty years saw what I did</u>.*
> *That is why [dio] I was angry with that generation,*
>   *and I said, 'Their hearts are always going astray,*
>   *and they have not known my ways.'*
> *So I declared on oath in my anger,*
>   *'They shall never enter my rest.'"*

For Hebrews, the forty-year period is not defined by wrath, as in Psalm 95, but by God's activity, his works. Anger is what *follows* this forty-year period *if* his readers do not rid themselves of "a sinful, unbelieving heart" (Heb. 3:12).

Again, the writer of Hebrews uses Psalm 95 as part of a larger argument in this section. He says that Jesus is the new and better Moses. He also draws the analogy between Israel and the church. As Moses led his people out of slavery into the desert to bring them to the promised land, Jesus led his people out of slavery and into the desert to bring them to another promised land. The difference is that with Jesus, the people are not Israel but the church; the slavery is not to Pharaoh but to Satan and sin; the promised land is not Canaan, but "a better country—a heavenly one" (Heb. 11:16).

To be consistent, this analogy must account for the forty-year desert period; if Israel had a forty-year wilderness journey before entering their rest, the church has one as well. And what corresponds to Israel's forty years between deliverance and promised land? The church's "wilderness wandering" is simply its existence as God's people, having been redeemed but now awaiting the final stage of the journey, the final rest (Heb. 4:1–11). The problem with this analogy, however, is that for Israel, the forty years is a period of *wrath*; it is their *punishment* time for their rebellion. This *cannot* be the way to describe the existence of the church. The church is the manifestation of God's *blessing*, not punishment. Because the analogy breaks down, the author of Hebrews adjusts the psalm in order to reflect the realities of Christ's work.

That such a move was intentional on the part of the author seems clear in light of Hebrews 3:17: "And with whom was he *angry for forty years*?" Here, Hebrews cites Psalm 95 "correctly": forty years is the period of God's *anger*. Why does he cite the same passage in two different ways just a few verses from each other? Was it because his conscience suddenly began to bother him? ("I departed from grammatical-historical exegesis in 3:10, but I'd better get back to it in 3:17.") The reason he cites the psalm differently is that in 3:17 he is talking about *Israel*, while in 3:10 he is talking about the *church*. In 3:17, the author is looking back to the original context of the psalm, and so he cites it the way it was intended. In order for the psalm to be read as a Christian psalm, however, some changes need to be made. And to stress the point again, however much we might frown upon this interpretive method, it is clear that the author of Hebrews knew exactly what he was doing. It is also clear that such an interpretive move would not have aroused the slightest bit of suspicion on the part of his readers.

These five examples (plus Luke 20:34–38, discussed earlier in the chapter) give a brief, but accurate, view of some of the interpretive methods employed by the New Testament writers. But we must also look at another dimension of apostolic hermeneutics, the interpretive *traditions* they adopted that were current in their day.

Apostolic Hermeneutics as a Second Temple Phenomenon: Interpretive Traditions

We saw above that the Wisdom of Solomon retold the Old Testament story to its readers and in doing so incorporated many preexisting interpretive traditions. Although the New Testament does not have many examples of such lengthy retellings (although see Acts 7 and Heb. 11), we see many places in the New Testament where writers likewise incorporate such traditions in references to Old Testament episodes. These traditions are not incorporated intentionally by the New Testament writers in an effort to connect with their audience; that is, it is not that the apostles "knew better" but were simply joining in for the benefit of their less enlightened readers. Rather, these traditions seem to represent the biblical authors' own *understanding* of these Old Testament episodes. As we saw in the Wisdom of Solomon, these interpretive traditions are referred to in a shorthand manner. Also, for the most part, they are rather incidental to the surrounding context.

Far from demonstrating their unimportance, the brevity and incidental nature of these interpretive comments demonstrate the degree to which these traditions were part of the common discourse about the Bible—*even* for the inspired New Testament writers. But, if we appeal to the incarnational analogy, this should come as no surprise. In order to communicate with their audience, we should expect the New Testament authors to do nothing different. Instead of their reinterpretation of certain texts being an embarrassing problem, it is simply another demonstration of the degree to which God's word is couched in terms familiar to the culture in which it is given.

Jannes and Jambres

A very clear example is 2 Timothy 3:8, where Paul refers to the magicians of Pharaoh's court by name as Jannes and Jambres:

> Just as Jannes and Jambres opposed Moses, so also these men oppose the truth—men of depraved minds, who, as far as the faith is concerned, are rejected.

These names do not come to us from the Old Testament but from the Second Temple interpretive world of which Paul was a part. The name *Jannes* is found in the Qumran scroll referred to as the Covenant of Damascus (5.17–19). Both names are found in *Targum Pseudo-Jonathan* to Exodus 1:15. Paul is not dropping these names to connect with Timothy's faulty notions of Old Testament content. These names were firmly in circulation in Paul's day. That Paul mentions these figures is not to be understood by us today as a historical declaration. It is, rather, an indication of what constituted Paul's "interpreted Bible."

Noah, the Preacher of Righteousness

Peter refers to Noah as "a preacher of righteousness" in 2 Peter 2:5. Such a description seems innocent enough, but when you stop to think about it, what exactly is Peter referring to? No such activity is attributed to Noah in the Old Testament, so why would Peter say it? This is a difficult question to answer if we isolate Peter from his Second Temple environment. The fact of the matter, however, is that a similar depiction of Noah as one who attempted to persuade his contemporaries to repent is found in several ancient sources, including Josephus's *Jewish Antiquities* 1.3.1. §74. Much of this work is an extended retelling of the Old Testament for the benefit of Josephus's Roman audience. And, as with other such Second Temple retellings of Scripture, Josephus includes preexisting interpretive traditions like this one. Others sources are a bit later: **Sibylline Oracles** 1.125–95 and a portion of the Babylonian Talmud (tractate *Sanhedrin* 108a).

How this tradition originated is, as always, largely a matter of conjecture. One explanation pertains to Noah being called "righteous" twice in the Genesis narrative. In Genesis 6:9 we read that Noah is righteous and blameless, and this presumably qualified him to be chosen as the deliverer of humanity. Then, after the ark is built, God says to Noah, "I have found you righteous in this generation" (7:1). For early interpreters of the Bible, this was no mere repetition: it provided an opportunity to dig a bit further. The question might have arisen, "What is it that Noah did to lead God to say *after* the ark was built, 'I have *found* you righteous in this generation'? Didn't we just read in 6:9 that Noah *was* righteous? We already know this, so why repeat it?" The answer might have been found in a story that described what Noah did *while he was building the ark*. It presumably took a lot of time, even though Genesis does not give start and completion dates. But a truly righteous man would not build such an ark and hoard it for himself and his family. He would have told others, preached to them, called them to repentance.

This is just one explanation, and if it does not help, it can be safely ignored. The larger point remains: Peter refers to Noah in a way that has no explicit biblical support but is found in other ancient sources. Peter is not working on his own here. His allusion to Noah's preaching activity is too brief to have generated the subsequent *Jewish* interpretive activity of the sources mentioned above. Rather, Peter's statement seems to be a very early witness to this ancient tradition.

The Dispute over Moses' Body

The dispute over Moses' body, mentioned nowhere in the Old Testament, is mentioned in Jude 9:

> But even the archangel Michael, when he was disputing with the devil about the body of Moses, did not dare to bring a slanderous accusation against him, but said, "The Lord rebuke you!"

What is striking about this statement, coupled with its not being found in the Old Testament, is that it enters Jude's flow of thought so innocently, so matter-of-factly.

Where did Jude get this? One could argue that this piece of information was given to him as a special revelation from God. Such an argument might be designed to protect the biblical author against the charge of simply making something up and reporting something that is not fact. So, as the logic goes, even though the episode concerning Moses' body is not in the Old Testament, it must have happened because Jude says it did.

The instincts of such an approach are both worthy and understandable, and I am sympathetic toward attempts to defend the Bible against these types of accusations, but this line of defense will not do. For one thing, if this is a special dose of revelation given to Jude, he does a good job of covering up that fact. He does not announce it as such, nor does he hint, "Here comes a piece of information you do not know but God revealed to me." Rather, it has an "as we all know" quality to it. It is presented as a *well-known* illustration to support Jude's argument. Jude is warning his readers about the influence of certain "godless men" (v. 4) among them. In verse 8 he describes them as "dreamers" who "pollute their own bodies, reject authority and slander celestial beings." It is in this context that Jude brings in the story of Moses' body—again, not as a special bit of knowledge, but as something he and his readers already knew. If the illustration were a new piece of information, then using it to support Jude's warning would have little force. Jude here is not a mouthpiece for new revelation from God. He is, as so often elsewhere in the New Testament, a conduit for an already existing interpretive tradition.

The original source of this story remains a debated topic. It may have originated as a way of explaining Deuteronomy 34:6: "To this day no one knows where his [Moses'] grave is." Could we really expect that the Israelites would have forgotten where they buried Moses? For modern interpreters, Deuteronomy 34:6 indicates that a considerable length of time elapsed between the death of Moses and the completion of the Pentateuch. But for early interpreters, such mundane (and modern) solutions would have held little attraction, and so a story was invented to account for this curious biblical comment. Whatever the roots of this tradition may be, however, we do know that Jude was not alone in this comment. Third-century church fathers Clement of Alexandria and Origen, among other early Christian writers, attributed this episode to the **Assumption of Moses** (also called the *Testament of Moses*). The extracanonical origin of Jude's comment is beyond debate. The better question is what Christians with a high view of Scripture should make of this fact.

Jude and 1 **Enoch**

Jude 14–15 cites a portion of prophecy supposedly uttered by Enoch, which is found in the noncanonical book *1 Enoch* but not in the Old Testament. The attribution of Jude 14–15 to *1 Enoch* 1.9 is universally accepted:

Enoch, the seventh from Adam, prophesied about these men: "See, the Lord is coming with thousands upon thousands of his holy ones to judge everyone, and to convict all the ungodly of all the ungodly acts they have done in the ungodly way, and of all the harsh words ungodly sinners have spoken against him." (Jude 14–15)

Behold, he will arrive with ten million of the holy ones in order to execute judgment upon all. He will destroy the wicked ones and censure all flesh on account of everything that they have done, that which the sinners and the wicked ones committed against him. (*1 Enoch* 1.9)

Why would Jude, an inspired canonical author, cite an uninspired noncanonical book? One answer is that Jude is merely using *1 Enoch* for illustrative purposes. In other words, he knows better than to think *1 Enoch* is "true." He is appealing to it, much like a modern preacher might quote C. S. Lewis from the pulpit. The problem with this explanation, however, is that Jude is referring to something that concerns the Bible directly. He is not saying, "As that revered theologian, the writer of *1 Enoch* says." He is saying, "As we all know, Enoch prophesied as follows," and then says something very similar to what is found in *1 Enoch* but, to our knowledge, nowhere else.

Jude did not have what we know as *1 Enoch* in front of him. The entire work grew from before the time of Christ until the early medieval period. Much of this book has pre-Christian origins, however, but that still does not imply that Jude had read these portions or even knew they existed. But deciding this issue is not all that important. What is less conjectural is that Jude quotes something that Enoch supposedly said that is not found in the Old Testament but is found in another ancient source.

The real issue is not that we have a canonical author citing a noncanonical text authoritatively. The more important issue is the *traditions* about Enoch that were in circulation and to which early interpreters—including Jude—had access. What is different about this example is that the traditions about Enoch were preserved in an independent work. The reason that Enoch generated a lot of interpretive activity may be because his biblical portrait raised a lot of questions. He was a mysterious Old Testament figure, someone who "walked with God; then was no more, because God took him away" (Gen. 5:24). There was clearly something special about him, and early interpreters went about the task of filling in gaps on this attractive biblical figure. Jude and *1 Enoch* bear witness to this.

Moses' Egyptian Education

Acts 7:21–22 makes a passing reference to Moses' Egyptian education:

> When he [Moses] was placed outside, Pharaoh's daughter took him and brought him up as her own son. Moses *was educated in all the wisdom of the Egyptians and* was powerful in speech and action.

What we read here in Stephen's speech is not explicit in the Old Testament, although perhaps it is implied in Exodus 2. After all, Moses was raised in Pharaoh's house, and it is not at all a stretch in logic to presume that he was therefore educated as an Egyptian.

The question is why anyone would feel the need to make this explicit in the context of Stephen's speech. The question is even more pressing when we note that the reference to Moses' education is hardly central to Stephen's theme. He is simply recounting Moses' early life (Acts 7:20–38). In these verses we read of many things taken directly from the Old Testament narrative: Moses' being hidden for three months after his birth; his being raised by Pharaoh's daughter; his confronting the Egyptian who mistreated an Israelite; his flight to Midian; his first meeting with God on Mount Sinai; the exodus.

Tucked into this rehearsal of Moses' life and work is the incidental comment about Moses' Egyptian education. The phrase in italic type in the citation above could simply be left out and nothing would be lost to the overall purpose of the speech. But it is there, not because Stephen wanted to add a nice little flourish, a bit of cleverness to show how interesting an interpreter of the Bible he was. It is there because it is part of Stephen's bare-boned outline of Moses' life.

The reference to Moses' education, although reasonable in terms of the actual biblical story, is not at all an explicit element of that story. For such an unimportant element in Exodus to be displayed so matter-of-factly in Stephen's speech must owe its existence to more than the off-the-cuff musings of the writer of Acts. Rather, Moses' Egyptian education is a topic of discussion in at least two ancient texts, both of which precede the New Testament: (1) Philo's *Life of Moses* 1.5 §§21–24, where the infant Moses showed such intellectual promise that teachers arrived from Egypt and Greece, and in short time he advanced beyond their learning, mastering subjects such as arithmetic, geometry, poetry, music, and astrology; and (2) an ancient play by "Ezekiel the Tragedian," *Exagōgē* lines 36–38 (second century BC).

Both of these sources refer to Moses' education. In the opinion of some scholars, the likely motivation for this tradition was apologetic, that is, to make Moses out to be highly educated, so that the Jews could boast to the Greeks that their tradition also had its philosopher. This would not have been a daring interpretive move. Since he was raised in Pharaoh's court, we would expect him to have been trained in all the wisdom of Egypt. And perhaps he was, but the point is that the Old Testament is completely silent about this. Acts 7:22 says what it says, however, because Second Temple interpreters were not silent.

The Law Was Put into Effect through Angels

Three times in the New Testament reference is made to angels playing some role in the giving of the law:

What, then, was the purpose of the law? It was added because of trans-
gressions until the Seed to whom the promise referred had come. *The law
was put into effect through angels by a mediator.* (Gal. 3:19)

Was there ever a prophet your fathers did not persecute? They even killed
those who predicted the coming of the Righteous One. And now you have
betrayed and murdered him—you who have received *the law that was put
into effect through angels* but have not obeyed it. (Acts 7:52–53)

For if *the message spoken by angels* was binding, and every violation and
disobedience received its just punishment, how shall we escape if we
ignore such a great salvation? (Heb. 2:2–3)

(Even though law is not mentioned specifically in the last passage, I
include this text since the reference to disobedience and punishment
seems to imply the law clearly enough.)

This tradition has no direct support in the Old Testament, though some
try to argue that it is anchored in Deuteronomy 33:2–4, which speaks
of God coming from Mount Sinai "with myriads of holy ones" (33:2).
Appeal is made to this passage by evangelicals wishing to exonerate the
New Testament authors from the charge of making things up. It may be
that this passage has something to do with the ultimate origins of this
tradition (for example, see *Targum Onqelos* to Deut. 33:2), but that is a
long way from saying that the New Testament authors were consciously
exegeting this passage in complete isolation from their hermeneutical
world and reproducing its sense.

Moreover, Deuteronomy 33:2–4 does not say that the law was put
into effect through angels, only that God came from Sinai (also Seir
and Mount Paran; see 33:2) with his "myriads of holy ones." These "holy
ones" are not angels but the Israelites, as 33:2–4 makes clear:

> The LORD came from Sinai
>   and dawned over them from Seir;
>   he shone forth from Mount Paran.
> He came with *myriads of holy ones*
>   from the south, from his mountain slopes.
> Surely it is you who love the *people*;
>   all the *holy ones* are in your hand.
> At your feet they all bow down,
>   and from you receive instruction,
> the law that Moses gave us,
>   the possession of the assembly of Jacob.

The "holy ones" are the Israelites who, after receiving the law from God, come down with God from Sinai. For any interpreter, modern or ancient, to appeal to Deuteronomy 33:2–4 to support a notion of angels mediating the law is an indication of what they wish to find there, not what *is* there.

I do not think the New Testament writers are inventing this idea, nor do I think that they are exegeting Deuteronomy 33:2–4 or any other Old Testament passage. Whatever the point of origin for this interpretation, the New Testament passages cited above should be placed in their Second Temple context. Perhaps something of that context can be seen in the book of *Jubilees*, where angels are referred to as being present with God on Mount Sinai. In *Jubilees* 1.27–29, the angel of the presence is instructed to write down for Moses the history of Israel from creation to the building of the sanctuary. In fact, the entire contents of *Jubilees* (which spans from creation to Sinai) is purported to have been spoken to Moses on Mount Sinai by the angel of the presence (*Jubilees* 2.1). I am not suggesting that the New Testament authors derived their statement directly from *Jubilees*. I find that extremely unlikely. My only point is that angelic activity between Moses and God on Sinai is not a biblical notion but, for whatever reason, a Second Temple one.

What is very important for us to see is how the reference to this tradition functions in the biblical passages cited above. Nothing here strikes one as being particularly innovative on the part of the New Testament authors. These are passing references to something that both the authors and readers simply accepted. This is especially noticeable in Acts 7:53. The purpose of Stephen's speech is to rehearse Israel's long history, focusing first on Abraham, then Joseph, and finally Moses and the exodus. Specifically, his speech is designed to recount Israel's rebellion and how those who crucified Christ are just as bad (see 7:51–53). It is here, at the end of the speech, that Stephen makes a passing reference to the law being put into effect through angels. As with Moses' Egyptian education, it really adds nothing to his argument. It is simply an example of a biblical author talking about an Old Testament episode *as he understood it*, that is, in terms of the interpretive traditions that formed his own unintentional notions of what was "in" the Bible, and also in the minds of some of his contemporaries.

Paul's Moveable Well

Our last example is more challenging. In 1 Corinthians 10, Paul warns his readers to stand firm in the face of temptation (10:12). He does so by looking back at Israel's period of wilderness wandering. He then makes a curious comment in 10:4 (italic type):

> For I do not want you to be ignorant of the fact, brothers, that our fore-
> fathers were all under the cloud and that they all passed through the sea.
> They were all baptized into Moses in the cloud and in the sea. They all
> ate the same spiritual food and drank the same spiritual drink; for they
> drank from the spiritual rock *that accompanied them*, and that rock was
> Christ. (1 Cor. 10:1–4)

Paul is no doubt referring here to the rock that provided water for
the Israelites mentioned in Exodus 17 and Numbers 20. By referring
to spiritual food and drink, Paul is using this Old Testament story to
make his point to his readers: the food and drink in the Old Testament are symbols of the spiritual sustenance that God provides for
his people through all time. And that spiritual sustenance for Paul's
readers is the very same Christ who sustained the Israelites in the
desert.

What is striking, however, is the comment that the rock that provided
this spiritual drink is said to have *accompanied* the Israelites through
the desert. What does this mean? When we place Paul's incidental
comment here side by side with other ancient texts, a picture begins to
emerge. Other Second Temple texts refer to a mobile source of water
accompanying the Israelites through the desert. Actually, there are
some variations on this story, but what they all have in common is
the notion of mobility. One example is *Targum Onqelos* to Numbers
21:16–20. This complex passage involves some interesting maneuvers
with the Hebrew text and so is beyond the scope of this book. (Interested readers can look at my article on the moveable well, listed at
the end of this chapter.) It speaks of the well dug in Numbers 21:18
as accompanying the Israelites on their journeys into the valleys and
mountains. No rock is mentioned, but the mobility of the source of
water is interesting nevertheless.

Another similar example is in a rabbinic text called the Tosefta, a
compilation of rabbinic traditions that predates the Talmud. Hence,
it is relatively old and therefore closer to the time of the New Testament. This text (found in the tractate *Sukkah* 3.11) speaks specifically
of a rock that went with the Israelites into the mountains and valleys;
wherever the Israelites camped, there was the rock. Both the Targum
and the Tosefta have fairly elaborate versions of this tradition that
contrast with the brevity (one word!) of Paul's account. Some suggest,
therefore, that Paul's statement cannot be connected in any meaningful way with these later texts, since Paul could not have copied from
texts written generations, even centuries, after he lived. The chronology is obviously true, but we must remember that the issue here is not
whether Paul plagiarized rabbinic texts. Rather, that Paul can make

such a brief, offhand comment about a moveable rock speaks to the existence, in some form, of a "moveable well" tradition already in Paul's day, so much so that he can make such a truncated comment and expect to be understood.

Another version of this tradition is found in the *Book of Biblical Antiquities*, a text much closer to Paul's day, which we glimpsed earlier with respect to Pseudo-Solomon's comments on Abraham. Containing two references to this tradition that should enter into the equation, this text speaks of a "well of water" that "follows" the Israelites through the desert:

> Now he [Moses] led his people out into the wilderness; for forty years he rained down for them bread from heaven and brought quail to them from the sea and brought forth *a well of water to follow them*. (10.7)

> And there [in the desert] he commanded him [Moses] many things and showed him the tree of life, from which he cut off and took and threw into Marah, and the water of Marah became sweet. *And it* [*the water*] *followed them in the wilderness forty years and went up to the mountain with them and went down into the plains*. (11.15)

What might have led to the creation of a tradition of a rock providing a mobile source of water? In addition to some of the Hebrew details addressed in *Targum Onqelos* and the Tosefta, another factor may be responsible. The rock that supplied water is mentioned twice in the Old Testament, in Exodus 17 and Numbers 20, that is, at the beginning and toward the end of the wilderness period. Early interpreters may have equated the two: they are the same rock. Hence, for the rock to have gone from Rephidim in Exodus 17 to Kadesh in Numbers 20, that rock must have rolled along with the Israelites throughout their forty-year wilderness period.

Should Paul's comment be understood as another example of this tradition? I think that is beyond a reasonable doubt. These other versions, even though they are later than Paul, are too elaborate to have been caused by Paul's incidental comment. Rather, Paul's incidental comment would have no meaning unless there was in existence a well-known tradition of a mobile source of water to back it up. Both Paul and the other texts are witnesses to an interpretive tradition that preceded both of them. By calling the rock Christ, Paul is certainly Christianizing this Old Testament story. But Paul's Old Testament is one that has already been subject to a rich history of interpretation. It is not just the words on the page but the interpretive tradition as well that made up Paul's Old Testament.

What Makes Apostolic Hermeneutics Unique?

The New Testament is similar to other Second Temple texts in two respects: the interpretive methods used and the interpretive traditions they adopt. This is not to say, however, that the New Testament is no different from these texts. Sometimes evangelical scholars try to put distance between the New Testament and its hermeneutical world by arguing that the apostles certainly did *some* of the things these other interpreters did but that they did so with much more restraint or balance. There may be some truth to this, but it hardly tells the whole story. The fact remains that time and time again the New Testament authors do some odd things, by our standards, with the Old Testament, but these things can be explained by taking note of the interpretive context in which the New Testament writers lived.

You cannot get to the heart of the uniqueness of the New Testament by driving a wedge between it and its Second Temple context. *How* the New Testament authors engaged the Old Testament (their interpretive methods) plus their own understanding of certain Old Testament passages (their adoption of preexisting interpretive traditions) certainly speak to the New Testament authors' *cultural* moment. But to ask *why* they engaged the Old Testament as they did begins to get at what makes apostolic hermeneutics unique. The driving force behind their Old Testament interpretations was their belief that Jesus of Nazareth was God with us and that he had been raised from the dead. It was, as mentioned earlier, their belief that the eschaton had come *in Christ*.

This is certainly similar to the Dead Sea community but with one important difference. The founder of the Christian community was "God with us," worker of miracles and sin's atonement, whom God vindicated by raising from the dead. Apostolic hermeneutics was driven by a Spirit-initiated intimacy with the crucified and risen Christ. It was their conviction that Christ was God's deliverer—a conviction that can come only by God's gift of illumination—as demonstrated in his crucifixion and resurrection, that drove the apostles to see all of the Old Testament as finding its culmination in Christ. The apostles did not arrive at the conclusion that Jesus is Lord from a dispassionate, objective reading of the Old Testament. Rather, they began with what they knew to be true—the historical death and resurrection of the Son of God—and on the basis of that fact reread their Scripture in a fresh way.

There is no question that such a thing can be counterintuitive for a more traditional evangelical doctrine of Scripture, since this is *eisegesis* (reading meaning *into* Scripture) rather than *exegesis* (getting meaning *from* Scripture). It is precisely a dispassionate, unbiased, objective reading that is normally considered to constitute valid reading. But what may be considered valid today cannot be the determining factor for understanding what the apostles did.

Another way of putting the problem is that apostolic hermeneutics violates what is considered to be a fundamental interpretive principle: don't take things out of context. So, it is thought, we cannot have New Testament writers taking the Old Testament out of context. But we must learn to look at it differently. It is not that the Old Testament words are taken out of context and tossed into the air to fall where they may. Rather, the New Testament authors take the Old Testament out of *one* context, that of the original human author, and place it into *another* context, the one that represents the final goal to which Israel's story has been moving.

To think of some of our examples above, it is difficult indeed to view Jesus coming out of Egypt in Matthew 2:15 as an objective reading of Hosea 11:1. The same holds for Paul's use of Isaiah 49:8 in 2 Corinthians 6:2 ("Now is the day of salvation"). Neither Matthew nor Paul arrived at his conclusion *from* reading the Old Testament. Rather, they began with the event from which all else is now to be understood. *The reality of the risen Christ drove them to read the Old Testament in a new way*: "Now that I see how it all ends, I can see how this part of the Old Testament, too, drives us forward."

As an analogy, it is helpful to think of the process of reading a good novel the first time and the second time. The two readings are not the same experience. Who of us has not said during that second reading "I didn't see that the last time," or "So *that's* how the pieces fit together." That the Old Testament is not a novel should not diminish the value of the analogy: the first reading of the Old Testament leaves you with hints, suggestions, trajectories, and so on, of how things will play out in the end, but it is not until you get to the end that you begin to see how the pieces fit together. And in that second reading, you also begin to see how parts of the story that seemed wholly unrelated at first now take on a much richer, deeper significance.

If Matthew were transported back in time and told Hosea that Hosea's words would be fulfilled in the boy Jesus and that, furthermore, this Jesus would be crucified and rise for God's people, I am not sure if Hosea would have known what to make of it. But if Hosea were to go forward to Matthew's day, it would be very different for him. There Hosea would be forced, in light of recent events, to see his words—precisely because they are inspired by God, the divine author—in the final *eschatological* context. In a stunning reversal, it is now *Matthew* who would show *Hosea* how his words fit into God's ultimate redemptive goal: the death and resurrection of Christ. And so Hosea's words, which in their original historical context (the intention of the human author, Hosea) did not speak of Jesus of Nazareth, now do.

The term I prefer to use to describe this eschatological hermeneutic is **christotelic**. I prefer this over *christological* or *christocentric* since these are susceptible to a point of view I am not advocating here, namely, needing to "see Christ" in every, or nearly every, Old Testament passage. *Telos* is the Greek word for "end" or "completion." To read the Old Testament "christotelically" is to read it *already knowing* that Christ is somehow the *end* to which the Old Testament story is heading.

To see Christ as the driving force behind apostolic hermeneutics is not to flatten out what the Old Testament says on its own. A grammatical-historical reading of the Old Testament is not only permissible but absolutely vital in that it allows the church to see the varied trajectories set in the pages of the Old Testament itself. It is only by understanding the Old Testament on its own terms, so to speak, that the church can appreciate the impact that the death and resurrection of Christ and the preaching of the gospel had in its first-century setting—and still should have today. But for the church, it is vital to remember that the Old Testament does not exist simply on its own, for its own sake. It cannot stand in isolation from the completion of the Old Testament story in the death and resurrection of Christ.

The Old Testament is a story, compiled over time, that is going somewhere, which is what the apostles are at great pains to show. It is the Old Testament as a whole, particularly in its grand themes, that finds its *telos*, its completion, in Christ. This is not to say that the vibrancy of the Old Testament witness now comes to an end, but that—on the basis of apostolic authority—it finds its proper goal, purpose, *telos*, in that event by which God himself determined to punctuate his covenant: Christ. What constitutes a Christian reading of the Old Testament is that it proceeds to the second reading, the eschatological, christotelic reading—and this is precisely what the apostles model for us.

In all this we need to consider another factor: the Old Testament story is fulfilled not only in Christ but in the new people of God. The coming of Christ, as the church claims, is the central event in the entire human story. The implications of that event included the giving of the Spirit at Pentecost and the formation of a new people of God, the church, where now Jew and Gentile, slave and free, male and female, become one people of God. Whatever racial, class, or gender distinctions might have been operative beforehand now count for nothing. A new world has begun where a Spirit-created people of God is formed into a new humanity, a humanity that lives and worships as one and as such fulfills, at least provisionally, the ideal lost in the garden.

In other words, there is not only a christotelic dimension to apostolic hermeneutics but an *ecclesiotelic* dimension as well: the apostolic use of the Old Testament does not focus exclusively on the *person* of Christ, but also on the *body* of Christ, his people, the church (Greek *ekklēsia*, literally "called-out ones"). For example, we saw in Galatians 3 that the church is Abraham's "seed"; that is, the people of God are being redefined by faith in Christ, by "belonging" to him (3:29). In making such a statement, Paul is not merely applying passages like Genesis 12:7 to the life of the church. He is saying that the *telos* of Genesis 12:7 is realized in the church. To put it another way, the ecclesiotelic dimension of Genesis 12:7 is an *extension* of the christotelic fulfillment. The story of Abraham has its *telos* in the church (we are Abraham's seed; Gal. 3:29) only because Christ completes the story first (he is Abraham's seed; Gal. 3:16).

We can see another example of this in Romans 15:1–4. Here Paul exhorts the strong to "bear with the failings of the weak." To make his point, he cites Psalm 69:9 ("The insults of those who insult you have fallen on me") and continues his argument: "For everything that was written in the past was written to teach us." Although at first blush this may seem to suggest a direct (moralistic?) application of an Old Testament text to the life of the Christian, a closer look tells a different story. Paul does not cite Psalm 69:9 with respect to the church primarily, but with respect to Christ and how he *first* fulfills 69:9:

> We should all please our neighbors for their good, to build them up. For *even Christ* did not please himself but, as it is written: "The insults of those who insult you have fallen on me." For everything that was written in the past was written to *teach us*, so that through the endurance taught in the Scriptures and the encouragement they provide we might have hope. (Rom. 15:2–4 TNIV, italics added)

Paul's logic is (1) build up others; (2) this is what Jesus did; (3) here is Psalm 69:9 to show you what *Jesus* did; (4) therefore, this Scripture was written to teach *us* what to do. The conclusion that Psalm 69:9 was "written to teach" the church (the ecclesiotelic dimension) comes by *first* seeing 69:9 in its christotelic fullness: it was written to teach us *because* it is Christ who first brought this text into the life of the church.

I do not hesitate to point out that the christotelic and ecclesiotelic dimensions do not explain absolutely everything the New Testament writers do with the Old Testament. There is variety in how the apostles handled the Old Testament, and I have no desire to gloss over the fact. I maintain, however, that the shape of apostolic hermeneutics is best explained by bearing in mind the Second Temple world in which they thought and wrote, as well as the fundamental conviction that Jesus is the *telos* of the Old Testament. These factors are seen again and again on the pages of the New Testament.

It is far less strained and historically much more justifiable to explain apostolic hermeneutics in light of these factors than it is to impose onto the New Testament writers a hermeneutical grid we might be comfortable with but that has no real connection with their historical setting. Otherwise, we may find ourselves in the position of having to contort ourselves to explain apostolic hermeneutics according to standards that the apostles themselves did not adopt.

Should We Handle the Old Testament the Way the Apostles Did?

What do we do with all this information? It is not enough simply to take note of apostolic hermeneutics and then move it to the side. We must ask what we can learn from this about the nature of the Bible and what it means to interpret it today. This is an ongoing issue for the church, and I make no claim to have arrived at the final word here. I am more interested in allowing the data we just looked at to shape even the kinds of questions we ask of the Bible and then work out some of the answers. The matter of biblical interpretation should remain a topic of vibrant discussion for the church. Here are some implications that come to mind.

Perhaps the most pressing question is what role all this should play in the church's use of the Old Testament today, which brings us to the question of interpretive methods of the New Testament writers. The problem basically amounts to this:

1. If we follow the apostles, we may wind up handling the Old Testament in a way that violates some of our interpretive instincts.
2. If we don't follow them, we are either admitting that the New Testament authors were misguided in showing us how Jesus is connected to the Old Testament, or that their hermeneutic is theirs alone and cannot be reproduced today.

This is a *real* dilemma and there is no simple solution.

As mentioned earlier, one way out of this dilemma is to argue that the apostles were justified in their creative handling of Scripture because they were apostles, inspired by God, and thus had the authority to do so. Because we are not inspired, we must follow the sure path of grammatical-historical exegesis, which focuses on the original human author's intention as an objective anchor to interpretation. This approach is one way of supporting the first option mentioned at the beginning of this chapter: it recognizes apostolic authority but lifts from us the burden of having to handle the Old Testament the way they did.

But this also creates certain problems of its own. First, it would have to be explained what it is about apostolic authority that would justify their handling of Scripture in such odd ways. Does authority mean that you can violate supposedly basic rules of interpretation? Isn't it precisely the apostles' inspired, authoritative status that would demand they take God-breathed Scripture more seriously by not adding to it? This view amounts to saying "They are apostles, so we had better *not* follow their lead." One could just as easily argue that it is precisely *because* they were the apostles, to whom the inscripturation of the New Testament had been entrusted, that we *should* follow them. Whom *better* to follow? We follow them in their teaching, so why not in their hermeneutic? Otherwise, we might be tempted to impose on Scripture a hermeneutical standard that is essentially foreign to it, which is in fact what sometimes happens.

We must also remember what we learned from the Second Temple context. If anything is *not* a sign of their unique apostolic authority, it is in how the New Testament writers handled the Old Testament. Both their interpretive methods and interpretive traditions are well documented in other Second Temple texts. They do not interpret the Old Testament in odd ways because they are apostles and can do what they want. They do what they do because they are first-century biblical interpreters who are heirs to a long and vibrant history of interpretation. We cannot appeal to apostolic authority to avoid the problems caused by apostolic hermeneutics.

Two options can be safely jettisoned by evangelicals. The first is to dismiss apostolic hermeneutics as irrelevant to the church's present interpretive task: the apostles did what they did; we do what we do. Most Christians instinctively pull away from such an extreme position. The apostles surely have *something* to say about the Old Testament worth listening to! The other extreme should also be avoided: Simply copy what the apostles did at every turn. Say what they said about the specific Old Testament passages they cite. Be silent where they are silent, and where they are not, follow them to the letter. One problem with this approach is that it does not address the very real tensions created by apostolic hermeneutics for modern interpreters. Although we cannot allow modern standards to set the agenda, neither can we ignore the cultural distance between us and Second Temple interpreters.

Avoiding these extremes, there seem to be basically two general options open to us (with, of course, various nuances and variations):

1. Defend the apostles against the accusation that they are practicing the faulty hermeneutics of Second Temple Judaism and argue

that the New Testament's use of the Old Testament is essentially in harmony with grammatical-historical exegesis.
2. Acknowledge the Second Temple setting of apostolic hermeneutics but discern carefully what sorts of things can and cannot carry over to today.

The first seems to be the most prevalent evangelical response, but it can work only by isolating the New Testament from its Second Temple context and by expending a lot of mental energy lining up the New Testament's use of the Old Testament with the original context of the Old Testament passage cited. What is at work here is more an attempt to conform Scripture to predetermined ways of thinking than allowing Scripture to help shape how we think. The second approach generally represents my own and that of a significant number of other evangelicals, although there are variations within this broad perspective.

A very respected proponent of this position is Richard Longenecker. Basically, what he says is that we may follow the apostles where they treat the Old Testament in a manner consistent with what we call grammatical-historical exegesis, but only there. Where they show their dependence on Second Temple techniques, we cannot follow. In other words, he draws the distinction between different types of exegetical *methods* and argues that those more akin to grammatical-historical exegesis command our attention whereas those more suited to first-century cultural conventions do not. In my own assessment of Longenecker, it is hard not to see the common sense in such a proposal, on one level. We all feel an instinctive discomfort with people who interpret the Bible in ways that have no connection with its original context. Still, to limit apostolic authority in the way Longenecker does, it seems to me, amounts to not following the apostles in any meaningful sense. The ultimate standard is still *ours*, not theirs.

Rather than making a distinction between methods on the basis of a modern standard, I suggest that we distinguish between *hermeneutical goal* and *exegetical method*. The apostles' hermeneutical goal, the centrality of the death and resurrection of Christ, must also be ours because we share the same "eschatological moment," that is, we too live in the postresurrection universe. This is why we *must* follow them precisely with respect to their *christotelic hermeneutic*, that is, their Christ-centered attitude toward the Old Testament. But that means, quite clearly, that we cannot be limited to following them where they treat the Old Testament in a more literal fashion (Longenecker's argument), since the literal (first) reading will not lead the reader to the christotelic (second) reading.

A Christian understanding of the Old Testament should *begin* with what God revealed to the apostles and what they model for us: the centrality of the death and resurrection of Christ for Old Testament interpretation. We, too, are living at the end of the story; we—as were the apostles—are engaged in the second, christotelic reading by virtue of our eschatological moment, the last days, the inauguration of the eschaton. As we read and interpret, we bring the death and resurrection of Christ to bear on the Old Testament.

This is not a call to flatten out the Old Testament, so that every psalm or proverb speaks directly and explicitly of Jesus. It is to ask oneself, "What difference does the death and resurrection of Christ make for how I understand this part of the Old Testament?" Our privileged status to be living in the postresurrection cosmos *must* be reflected in our understanding of the Old Testament. Therefore, if what claims to be a Christian understanding of the Old Testament simply remains in the preeschatological moment—simply reads the Old Testament "on its own terms"—such is not a Christian understanding in the apostolic sense.

What then of the exegetical methods employed by the apostles? Here I feel the force of Longenecker's point: we do not live in the Second Temple world. What made sense back then would not necessarily make sense now. I have no hesitation in saying that I would feel extremely uncomfortable to see our pastors, exegetes, or Bible study leaders change, omit, or add words and phrases to make their point, even though this is what New Testament authors do. One very real danger that we are all aware of is how some play fast and loose with Scripture to support their own agendas. The church instinctively wants to guard against such a misuse of Scripture by saying, "Pay attention to the words in front of you in their original context." What helps prevent (but does not guarantee against) such flights of fancy is grammatical-historical exegesis.

But here is our dilemma. However much we might regard certain Second Temple interpretive methods and traditions as unworkable in our modern context, we still cannot simply fill the void by adopting the grammatical-historical method as the default and exclusively normative hermeneutic for modern Christians. Why? To lift up grammatical-historical exegesis as the ultimate standard means we must either (1) distance ourselves from the christotelic hermeneutic of the apostles or (2) mount arguments showing that apostolic hermeneutics is actually grounded in the grammatical-historical meaning of the Old Testament, and that all this talk about the Second Temple context is just nonsense that can be safely avoided. To adopt the first option means to distance ourselves from any real notion of apostolic authority. To adopt the second is untenable because the Second Temple evidence cannot be ignored—or better, it can be ignored only by means of a willful choice to disregard the plain evidence we have.

The way I begin to work through this impasse is to question what we mean by method. The word implies, at least to me, a worked-out, conscious application of rules and steps to arrive at a proper understanding of a text. But what if method, so understood, is not as central a concept for New Testament authors as we might think? What if their biblical interpretation was not guided so much by method but by an intuitive, Spirit-led engagement of Scripture, with the anchor being not what the Old Testament author intended but how Christ gives the Old Testament its final coherence? We may think that properly employing the right methods will yield the proper results. But perhaps, like the New Testament authors, we should think of the goal first and recognize that methods exist to serve that goal.

What drives apostolic hermeneutics is not adherence to a method. Rather, the coming of Christ is so climactic that it required the New Testament writers to look at the Old Testament in a whole new light. To speak of the apostles' exegetical methods may lead us down the wrong path to begin with. I do not mean to make sweeping statements against exegetical methods or grammatical-historical exegesis. But when we observe what the apostles did with their Scripture, we can only conclude that there must be more to Christian biblical interpretation than uncovering the original meaning of an Old Testament passage.

The New Testament writers were so consumed by Christ that their understanding of God's past actions was brought under the authority of God's present act, the climax of his covenant with Israel, the person and work of Christ. And so their minds were illumined to see what was largely hidden to the human authors of the Old Testament but was always the goal and intention of the divine author.

What We Can Learn from Apostolic Hermeneutics

Both the interpretive methods and the traditions employed by the New Testament writers were embedded in the Second Temple culture. The temptation might be to dismiss all this, since we live in a very different world. But there may be a lesson or two we can learn, to encourage us to be much more self-reflective about not only *how* we handle the Old Testament but, more importantly, *why*.

To understand the contextual nature of the apostles' interpretive activity helps us to see that God gave us the gospel not as an abstract doctrinal formulation, but already contextualized. Revelation necessarily implies a human context. When God speaks and acts, he does so within the human drama as it is expressed at a certain time and place and with all the cultural trappings that go along with it. This makes revelation somewhat messy, but it does not seem to work any other way. In fact, it would seem that God would not have it any other way. For the apostles to interpret the Old Testament in ways consistent with the hermeneutical expectations of the Second Temple world is analogous to Christ himself becoming a Second Temple citizen. If identifying Christ himself as a first-century Jew is the great demonstration of the lengths to which God will go to redeem his people, the great manifestation of God's love, is there any reason to shy away from identifying the New Testament, the written witness to Christ, as likewise defined by its first-century context?

And if this is true for God, it should remind us that our own understanding of the Old Testament—and the gospel—has a contextual dimension as well. As subjective as this sounds, it is nevertheless inescapable that (1) the historical contexts of the biblical authors played a determining role in the shape that God's revelation took, and (2) likewise our own historical moment plays a significant determining role in how we read and understand Scripture. If any of this is troublesome, it may be because we have not adequately grappled with the implications of God himself giving us Scripture in context. This should motivate us to greater humility about our own interpretive conclusions while at the same time inspiring us to greater depth and profundity as we engage the Old Testament in its christotelic fullness.

This should also remind us that biblical interpretation is at least as much art as it is science. The more I reflect on the nature of biblical interpretation throughout its long history—particularly apostolic hermeneutics—as well as in today's world, the more I am convinced that there must be more to the nature of biblical interpretation than simply uncovering the "meaning of the text," as if it were an objective exercise. Although we are to think christotelically about the Old Testament, there are multiple ways of expressing this. In other words, the Old Testament is open to multiple layers of meaning. I may not agree, for example, that Moses' raised hands in Exodus 17 are a sign of the cross. I may not agree that Rahab's red cord in Joshua 2 foreshadows the blood of Christ. But I must remember that, throughout church history, many have interpreted these passages in this way. As much as these interpretations may run up against my own hermeneutical sensibilities, I must nevertheless be willing to allow those sensibilities to be open to critique. Moreover, inasmuch as Scripture is the word of God, I would expect multiple layers of meaning insofar as no one person, school, or tradition can exhaust the depth of God's word.

I do not think that a Christian understanding of the Old Testament has taken place if the interpreter remains on the level of grappling with the Hebrew syntax or ancient Near Eastern context. That is merely one dimension of biblical interpretation. Christian proclamation must move well beyond the bounds of such scientific markers. In the end, what every preacher and interpreter knows instinctively is that the words that actually come out of their mouths are a product of much more than an exegetical exercise. Christian, apostolic proclamation of the Old Testament is a subtle interpenetration of a myriad of factors, both known and unknown, that can rightly be described not as a product of science but as a work of art. It includes such things as creativity, intuition, risk, and a profound sense of the meaningfulness of the endeavor, all centered on the commitment to proclaim that "Jesus is Lord."

Perhaps, then, we can also appreciate that biblical interpretation is at least as much community oriented as it is individually oriented. I sometimes speak with younger pastors or students who say, "I worked all week on this sermon." Others write exegetical papers for my classes that require research, but such research rarely goes back beyond several recent commentaries or articles. And it is a rarity indeed if they ask their fellow classmates for help (although they do tend to line up outside my door a day or two before the due date).

But biblical interpretation is a true community activity. It is much more than individuals studying a passage for a week or so. It is about individuals who see themselves as part of a community that reaches far back into history and extends to the many cultures across the world today. Truly, we are not islands of interpretive wisdom. We rely on the witness of the church through time (with the hermeneutical trajectory set by the apostles as a central component), as well as the wisdom of the church in our time—both narrowly considered as a congregation, denomination, or larger tradition and more broadly considered as a global reality, all of which involves the direct involvement of the Spirit of God. Biblical interpretation is not merely a task that individuals perform; it is something that grows out of our participation in the family of God in the broadest sense possible.

Perhaps we should think of biblical interpretation more as a path to walk than a fortress to be defended. Of course, there are times when defense is necessary, but the church's task of biblical interpretation should not be defined by such. I see regularly the almost unbearable burden we place on our preachers by expecting them, in a week's time, to read a passage, determine its meaning, and then communicate it effectively. The burden of "getting it right" can sometimes be discouraging and hinder effective ministry. I would rather think of biblical interpretation as a path we walk, a pilgrimage we take, whereby the longer we walk and take in the surrounding scenes, the more people we stop and converse with along the way, and the richer our interpretation will be. Such a journey is not always smooth. At times what is involved is a certain degree of risk and creativity: we may need to leave the main path from time to time to explore less traveled but promising tracks.

To be sure, our job is also to communicate the gospel in all its simplicity, but that does not mean that biblical interpretation is an easy task—the history of the church's interpretive activity should put such notions to rest. Biblical interpretation always requires patience and humility lest we stumble. We are not required to handle everything that comes our way, and the gospel will not crumble in the process. But as we attempt to understand Scripture, we move further along the path. At the end of the path is not simply the gaining of knowledge about the text, but God himself who speaks to us therein. The goal toward which the path is leading is that which set us on the path to begin with: our having been claimed by God as coheirs with the crucified and risen Christ. The reality of the crucified and risen Christ is both the beginning and end of Christian biblical interpretation.

Further Reading

Beale, G. K. *The Right Doctrine from the Wrong Text? Essays on the Use of the Old Testament in the New*. Grand Rapids: Baker, 1994.

> Balanced collection of classic essays on the topic. Beale himself essentially argues that the New Testament authors respected the context of the Old Testament writers.

Bruce, F. F. *Biblical Exegesis in the Qumran Texts*. Grand Rapids: Eerdmans, 1959.

> An excellent, readable introduction by the noted evangelical scholar.

Charlesworth, James H., ed. *The Old Testament Pseudepigrapha*. 2 vols. Garden City, NY: Doubleday, 1983–85.

> Translations and helpful introductions to each of the Pseudepigrapha, including such topics as historical, theological, and cultural importance.

Enns, Peter. "Apostolic Hermeneutics and an Evangelical Doctrine of Scripture: Moving beyond the Modernist Impasse." *Westminster Theological Journal* 65 (2003): 263–87.

> A more detailed version of some of the thoughts outlined in this chapter.

———. *Exodus Retold: Ancient Exegesis of the Departure from Egypt in Wis 10:15–21 and 19:1–9*. Harvard Semitic Museum Monographs 57. Atlanta: Scholars Press, 1997.

Contains more detailed explanations of Pseudo-Solomon's interpretation of
Exodus than discussed above.

———. "The 'Moveable Well' in 1 Corinthians 10:4: An Extra-biblical
Tradition in an Apostolic Text." *Bulletin for Biblical Research* 6 (1996):
23–38.

A defense of 1 Corinthians 10:4 as an example of the "moveable well tradition."

Evans, Craig A. *Noncanonical Writings and New Testament Interpretation*. Peabody, MA: Hendrickson, 1992.

Handy one-volume overview of Second Temple literature, including rabbinic
and gnostic writings.

Fishbane, Michael. *Biblical Interpretation in Ancient Israel*. Oxford: Clar-
endon, 1985.

Indispensable, scholarly treatment of the phenomenon of innerbiblical
interpretation.

Greidanus, Sidney. *Preaching Christ from the Old Testament: A Contemporary Hermeneutical Method*. Grand Rapids: Eerdmans, 1999.

Overview of the hermeneutical challenges to preaching Christ from the Old
Testament. Practical guide, with examples, that also tries to tackle the difficult
questions.

Hays, Richard. *Echoes of Scripture in the Letters of Paul*. New Haven:
Yale University Press, 1989.

Important contribution to the discussion of Paul's use of the Old Testament. It
is not simply the case that Paul uses the Old Testament, but that his letters are
imbued with echoes of the Old Testament. I am indebted to Hays for the term
ecclesiotelic.

Kugel, James L. *Traditions of the Bible: A Guide to the Bible As It Was at
the Start of the Common Era*. Cambridge: Harvard University Press,
1998.

Massive yet readable compilation of biblical stories and how they were
understood in the Second Temple period and into the medieval period. This
volume is a more detailed version of Kugel's previous, popular work, alluded to
in the subtitle: *The Bible As It Was*. The value of this work for students of
Second Temple interpretation is inestimable.

Kugel, James L., and Rowan A. Greer. *Early Biblical Interpretation*. Library of Early Christianity 3. Philadelphia: Westminster, 1986.

Popular introduction to Second Temple interpretation.

Longenecker, Richard N. *Biblical Exegesis in the Apostolic Period*. 2nd ed. Grand Rapids: Baker, 1999.

> Classic evangelical treatment. Must reading. Longenecker squarely settles the New Testament authors in their Second Temple interpretive world and draws some conclusions about how the church today can and cannot follow them.

McCartney, Dan G. "The New Testament's Use of the Old Testament." Pages 101–16 in *Inerrancy and Hermeneutic: A Tradition, a Challenge, a Debate*. Edited by H. Conn. Grand Rapids: Baker, 1988.

> Wonderful introduction to apostolic hermeneutics compared with that of Qumran. Argues that the interpretive method for both was subservient to the interpretive goal.

McCartney, Dan G., and Peter Enns. "Matthew and Hosea: A Response to John Sailhamer." *Westminster Theological Journal* 63 (2001): 97–105.

> Proposes that Matthew is not engaging Hosea on a grammatical-historical level. Response to Sailhamer's article (below).

Sailhamer, John. "Hosea 11:1 and Matthew 2:15." *Westminster Theological Journal* 63 (2001): 87–96.

> Defends Matthew's use of Hosea as following the "compositional clues" in Hosea.

VanderKam, James C. *The Dead Sea Scrolls Today*. Grand Rapids: Eerdmans, 1994.

> Concise and readable introduction to the Dead Sea Scrolls.

Vermes, Geza. *The Dead Sea Scrolls in English*. 4th ed. London: Penguin, 1995.

> A handy, one-volume translation of many of the more important Dead Sea Scrolls.

Wright, Christopher J. H. *Knowing Jesus through the Old Testament*. Downers Grove, IL: InterVarsity, 1992.

> Accessible introduction to understanding Jesus as the continuation and climax of Israel's story. Full of wonderful insights.

5

The Big Picture

What Is the Bible, and What Are We Supposed to Do with It?

To ask questions about the identity and purpose of the Bible might appear to be a bit over the top, not only at the end of a book but in general. One would have to be somewhat self-absorbed to think he or she can have anything final to say on what the Bible *is* and what we should *do* with it. Still, this book did not focus on giving the final word on any topic; I tried to help begin new conversations about Scripture, not end them, by advocating a more open and curious posture toward the challenges contemporary readers of the Bible face. No doubt, this means wrestling with the difficult question "How do we incorporate certain data with full integrity without sacrificing the truth that the Bible is God's book for his people?" I believe that the process of answering that question may be significantly aided for some by asking how the incarnation of Christ helps us to build a better model for the inspiration of Scripture.

Such an approach cannot help but have a provisional quality to it. As I mentioned at the very beginning, neither the issues addressed in this book (ancient Near Eastern evidence, theological diversity, and the New Testament's use of the Old Testament) nor the perspective from which I view them are novel. Interested readers can find similar ideas expressed much more fully in many other books, a very few of which are mentioned in the "Further Reading" sections. My aim throughout has been synthesis, not novelty, for people who have very good and difficult questions about the Bible but who may not have a theological paradigm from which to work through some of these questions.

To work within an incarnational paradigm means that our expectations of the Bible must be in conversation with the data, otherwise we run the very real risk of trying to understand the Bible in fundamental isolation from the cultures in which it was written—which is to say, we would be working with a very nonincarnate understanding of Scripture. Whatever words Christians employ to speak of the Bible (inerrant, infallible, authoritative, revelational, inspired), either today or in the past, must be seen as attempts to describe what can never be fully understood. I do not mean that the Bible is a complete mystery, that we have no meaningful way of speaking of it. I only mean that the incarnate written word (Scripture) is, like Christ, beyond our ability to grasp exhaustively: we can speak of the incarnate Christ meaningfully, but never fully. We should not think that the Bible, expressed as it is in the more tangible, controllable medium of human language, is any less mysterious. This is why the incarnational analogy is problematic on at least one level. The purpose of an analogy is to explain a lesser-known thing by using something better known. But the incarnation of Christ is itself precisely what needs explaining.

Perhaps, then, it makes more sense to speak of the incarnational *parallel* between Christ and the Bible. This should lead us to a more willing recognition that the expression of our confession of the Bible as God's word has a provisional quality to it. By faith, the church confesses that the Bible *is* God's word. It is up to Christians of each generation, however, to work out what that means and what words work best to describe it.

As to the question of the Bible's uniqueness, which is raised by the ancient Near Eastern evidence, it is certainly the case that the Bible is a book like no other, and "unique" is a very good word to describe it—provided that using this word does not prevent us from recognizing and *embracing* the marks of the ancient settings in which the Bible was written. Its uniqueness is seen not in holding human cultures at arm's length, but in the belief that Scripture is the only book in which God speaks incarnately. As it is with Christ, so it is with the Bible—the "coming together" of the divine and human sets it apart from all others.

That God willingly and enthusiastically participates in our humanity should give us pause. If even God expresses himself in the Bible through particular human circumstances, we must be very ready to see the necessarily culturally limited nature of our own theological expressions today. I am not speaking of cultural relativism, where all truth is up for grabs and the Bible ceases being our standard for faith. I simply mean that all of our theologizing, because we are human beings living in particular historical and cultural moments, will have a temporary and provisional—even fallen—dimension to it.

In other words, there is no absolute point of reference to which we have access that will allow us to interpret the Bible stripped of our own cultural context. We must avoid the extremes of (1) jettisoning our context and (2) becoming slaves to our context. We must learn to negotiate the tension between being inescapably creatures of time and space while at the same time remembering the church's prophetic responsibility of calling all cultures to obedience to the same gospel. And we issue this call not by holding the world in which we live at arm's length, but precisely by participating in that world—the world that God created, in which he has placed us.

Because our theologies are necessarily limited and provisional, the church today must be open to listening to how other Christians from other cultures read Scripture and live it out in their daily lives. In my own Christian experience I have found myself in places where I no longer represented the dominant Western culture, either through travel or interacting with international students. These kinds of experiences remind me that some issues have many sides, which then prompts me to examine how my own cultural context influences me to see some things but not others. Christians truly can and must learn from each other, which includes both give and take, acceptance and criticism. And we must learn to see this as a positive. That we are bound by time and place is not a sorry state of affairs that we simply have to put up with until we can learn to rise above it. The incarnational analogy helps us to see it differently: diverse expressions of God's one, but multidimensional, gospel are precisely what he wanted.

This brings us to our second topic, the theological diversity of the Old Testament. The presence of theological diversity does not mean that it lacks integrity or trustworthiness. It means that we must recognize that the data of Scripture lead us to conceive differently of how Scripture has integrity or is worthy of trust. Scripture may indeed "lack integrity" if we impose upon it standards that have little in common with how the Bible itself behaves. We trust the Bible, not because we can show that there is no diversity, but because we believe, by the gift of faith, in the one who gave Scripture to us. We are to place our trust in God who gave us Scripture, not in our own conceptions of how Scripture ought to be.

By doing so, we can grow in appreciation of how very involved God has been in the lives of his people, both then and now. It encourages us to look to the Bible not as a timeless rule book or owner's manual for the Christian life—so that we can lift verses here and there and apply them. It helps us to see that the Bible has a dynamic quality to it, for God himself is dynamic, active, and alive in our lives and in the life of his church. Although the Bible is clear on central matters of the faith, it is flexible in many matters that pertain to the day to day (which is seen most clearly in our discussion of Proverbs in chapter 3).

To put it more positively, the Bible sets trajectories, not rules, for a good many issues that confront the church. For example, the Bible may not tell you how to raise a family in detail, but sets broad trajectories for what an "in-Christ" family can look like. And different families in different contexts will enter into these trajectories in different ways and, therefore, express their commitment to Christ differently. This flexibility of application is precisely what is modeled for us in the pages of Scripture itself, as we saw in chapter 3. The theological effort it takes for us to work out Christian living today continues the trajectory of flexibility set out in Scripture itself. And this working out, or "enfleshing," of the gospel is an inescapable outcome of Scripture as God's incarnate word.

Finally, with respect to the New Testament's use of the Old Testament, what is modeled for us is that Christ is the goal of the Old Testament story, meaning that he is the ultimate focus of Christian interpretation. Not every verse or passage is about him in a superficial sense. Rather, Christ is the deeper sense of the Old Testament—at times more obvious than others—in whom the Old Testament drama as a whole finds its ultimate goal or *telos*. It is in the person and work of Christ that Christians seek to read the Old Testament, to search out how it is in Christ that the Old Testament has integrity, how it is worthy of trust, how the parts cohere. Such coherence is not found by superficially putting isolated pieces of the Old Testament together to make them fit somehow, but by allowing the tensions to remain and asking how our fuller knowledge of God's incarnational pattern can add to our reading of Scripture.

I am very intentional here in saying that this is something we *seek* after. A christotelic coherence is not achieved by following a few simple rules of exegesis. It is to be sought after, over a long period of time, in community with other Christians, with humility and patience. Biblical interpretation is, as mentioned in chapter 4, a path we walk rather than a fortress we defend. I am not ruling out, by any stretch of the imagination, an apologetic or evangelistic dimension of Scripture. I am saying that the primary purpose of Scripture is for the church to eat and drink its contents in order to understand better who God is, what he has done, and what it means to be his people, redeemed in the crucified and risen Son. Such an understanding of the purpose of Scripture—as a means of grace for the church—actually opens up possibilities of interpretation instead of closing them. Our task in biblical interpretation is to communicate the one, unchanging gospel—of what God, the creator and redeemer, has done in Christ—in such a way that respects and even *expects* that message to be articulated differently in different contexts.

There do not seem to be any clear rules or guidelines to prevent us from taking this process too far. But again, this is why the metaphor of journey or pilgrimage is so appealing. The path we walk may contain risks, unexpected bumps, twists, and turns. We do not always know what is coming around the corner—we were not able to anticipate the discovery of ancient Near Eastern creation texts or the Dead Sea Scrolls, for example. But yet, we have turned a few important corners over the past several generations. It is always an option, I suppose, to halt the journey and stand still, or perhaps turn around and walk back a few hundred yards, so as to stand at a safe distance from what lies ahead. We should continue the journey, however, not because we are sure of our own footing, but because we have faith in God who placed us on this journey to begin with.

Continuing the Conversation: Learning to Listen

With this in mind, I would like to conclude by looking at another important dimension of our discussion about Scripture. As concerned as I am that Christians sift through the evidence we have at our disposal, I am more concerned with *how* we carry on this conversation and *why*.

Although not universally true, many can attest that a strong element of suspicion exists among evangelicals both toward the types of evidence we have looked at and toward those who engage it. This is partly understandable, since a great deal of the history of modern biblical scholarship does not show evidence of being overly concerned with the doctrinal and practical implications of exegetical work. This is not a comment on the personal faith of these scholars, only that the necessary conversation between evidence and doctrine did not take place—or if it did, it was largely destructive.

But the evidence we have at our disposal transcends such labels as liberal or conservative. Evangelical biblical scholars and students of the Bible (which includes informal study as well as college or seminary) regularly find themselves having to interact with the important developments in recent generations. And this is why the suspicion needs to come to an end. I am not suggesting that we throw caution to the wind and bow to every trend. Part of the academic quest is to be critical of evidence until such time that certain conclusions seem to present themselves naturally. But the attitude of an academic quest is very different from judgmental suspicion, which is a predisposition against new and different ideas that challenge existing ones.

In some respects what drives this suspicion is fear that what is new will necessarily threaten the old, which is often uncritically equated with the gospel itself. I agree that modern biblical scholarship has handled some issues in ways that could certainly lead in that direction, and so fear is understandable. But fear cannot *drive* theology. It cannot be used as an excuse to ignore what can rightly be called evidence. We do not honor the Lord nor do we uphold the gospel by playing make-believe. Neither are those who engage the kinds of issues discussed in this book necessarily on the slippery slope to unbelief. Our God is much bigger than we sometimes give him credit for. It is we who sometimes wish to keep him small by controlling what can or cannot come into the conversation. The result is—what would have been soundly condemned by Christ himself and any New Testament writer—polarization and power plays among the people of God, the body of Christ, his ambassadors who are called by him to be his ministers of reconciliation to the world. The issue is not whether we disagree; that is healthy, provided it does not become an end in itself. The problem is that true Christians erect a wall of hostility between them, and churches, denominations, and schools split.

It has been my experience that sometimes our first impulse is to react to new ideas and vilify the person holding them, not considering that person's Christian character. We jump to conclusions and assume the worst rather than hearing—*really* hearing—each other out. What would be a breath of fresh air, not to mention a testimony to those around us, is to see an atmosphere, a culture, among conservative, traditional, orthodox Christians that models basic principles of the gospel:

- *Humility* on the part of scholars to be sensitive to how others will hear them and on the part of those whose preconceptions are being challenged.
- *Love* that assumes the best of brothers and sisters in Christ, not that looks for any difference of opinion as an excuse to go on the attack.
- *Patience* to know that no person or tradition is beyond correction, and therefore no one should jump to conclusions about another's motives.

How we carry on this very important conversation is a direct result of *why*. Ultimately, it is not about us, but about God. We must be very careful not to confuse God's kingdom with our own. We do not engage in biblical study to build our own private kingdoms; we do so because God in Christ has allowed us to co-labor with him in a kingdom he has already built. Jesus had a thing or two to say about having only one master, serving in only one kingdom, and those words translate well to theological matters. We are all susceptible to private kingdom building. Young students with newfound knowledge sometimes feel the freedom to throw off the shackles of their parents' faith and then crusade to help others go on that very same journey (the "angry evangelical" syndrome). Others rule over private kingdoms already well established, who in their arrogance have closed their hearts and minds to the continued work of God's Spirit.

We study the Bible so we can know better who God is and ultimately what he has done in Christ. Such study, by God's Spirit, is a means by which God forms us into the image of his risen Son, with whom we are coheirs. We must, therefore, be ever vigilant to inspect our own motives, lest we fall into the well-worn rut of thinking that study of the Bible prepares us to lead rather than to serve. It is to learn, after all is said and done, that the most important thing is not we who read the Bible, but he who gave it to us, in all its incarnate fullness.

Glossary

Akkadian—The major **Semitic language** in the ancient Near East during the third and second millennia BC. Unlike most of its neighboring languages (**Hebrew** being one of them), Akkadian has no alphabet. Rather, it is a syllabary, meaning that each Akkadian symbol represents a syllable. This makes for a very complex writing system, since there are potentially thousands of possible syllables in any language. (Think how many English syllables can be made just beginning with the letter *b*: ba, be, bi, bo, bu, bat, bet, etc.) Hence, literacy was not widespread, since only the educated could be expected to master such a writing system. The earliest evidence we have for a Semitic alphabet is of **Phoenician** origin and begins around 1700 BC. The Akkadian writing system is known as cuneiform, meaning wedge-shaped markings pressed into clay by means of a stylus.

Ammonites—The nation that descended from the second of two sons whom, according to Genesis 19:36–38, Lot's daughters bore him: **Moab** and Ben-Ammi. The Ammonites were located east of the Jordan River, north of Moab. Their history with the Israelites was largely contentious, as can be glimpsed in Deuteronomy 23:3 and 1 Samuel 11:1–11.

ANE—Common abbreviation for "ancient Near East(ern)." The term normally refers to the territories extending from the Mediterranean Sea eastward to the Tigris and Euphrates Rivers and beyond, but there are no universally agreed-upon precise geographical limitations. Depending on the context in which the term is used, it can also refer to Egypt, Persia (ancient Media and Elam), as well as the land of the Hittites (modern-day Turkey). Old Testament scholars typically use the term to refer to that part of the larger ancient world relevant to Israel.

Apocrypha—A collection of typically eighteen books that do not have canonical status for Jews and Protestants but are recognized as deuterocanonical (canonical, but of a secondary status) by Roman Catholicism and Eastern Orthodoxy. These books are three additions to Daniel (Bel and the Dragon, Prayer of Azariah and the Song of the Three Young Men, and Susanna), Additions to Esther, Baruch, 1–2 Esdras, Judith, Letter of Jeremiah, 1–4 Maccabees, Prayer of Manasseh, Psalm 151 (found among the Dead Sea Scrolls), Sirach (also called Ecclesiasticus), Tobit, and Wisdom of Solomon. Most of these works are of Greek origin and were written no earlier than the first half of the second century BC. These books contain much helpful information for understanding the political and religious world into which Jesus came. Some are also helpful in demonstrating the nature of biblical interpretation at that time.

Apostolic hermeneutics—A shorthand term to describe the manner in which Jesus and the New Testament authors interpreted the Old Testament. Apostolic hermeneutics, as I argue in this book, must be understood within the **hermeneutical** world of the **Second Temple period**.

Aramaic—The major language of international discourse during the first millennium BC, supplanting **Akkadian**. Like **Hebrew**, Aramaic is alphabetic, and it is very similar to Hebrew in many other respects as well (e.g., vocabulary, grammar). As a rough analogy, Aramaic and Hebrew are as similar as are German and Dutch. The popularity of Aramaic in the first millennium is reflected in the Old Testament itself. Portions of Ezra and Daniel were composed in Aramaic. It is also likely the main language spoken in Palestine in Jesus' day (see Mark 5:41; 15:34).

Asherah—A popular Canaanite goddess mentioned in numerous places in the Old Testament, mainly in the books of Kings. She is also known outside the Old Testament mainly from **Ugaritic** sources. She was worshiped in the form of a "tree" or wooden pole, hence the recurring biblical injunction to have them cut down (e.g., Exod. 34:13; Deut. 7:5; 1 Kings 15:13).

Assumption of Moses—Also known as the *Testament of Moses*, this text is generally dated to the first century AD, although the date is still debated in contemporary scholarship. The text purports to be a farewell speech given by Moses to Joshua (his successor) in which Moses tells Joshua what will happen to the Israelites from the entrance into Canaan to the end of time. This text illustrates the "testament" genre popular in the **Second Temple period**.

Assyrians—A nation whose roots go back to the third millennium BC but which became a dominant force only around 1700 BC. Their language was **Akkadian** or, more accurately, a dialect of Akkadian that itself developed and changed over the centuries, so that scholars speak, for example, of Old Assyrian (1950–1750 BC) and Neo-Assyrian (1000–625 BC). The Assyrian kings best known to readers of the Old Testament are probably Tiglath-pileser III (744–727 BC) and Shalmaneser V (726–722 BC). The former is the Assyrian king from whom King Ahaz of Judah sought help against enemy attack (2 Kings 16:7; Isa. 7:1–8:18). The latter attacked Samaria, the capital of the **northern kingdom**, and sent it into exile in 722 BC (2 Kings 18:9).

Baal—Canaanite storm and fertility god, referred to repeatedly in the Old Testament as a major threat to the worship of **Yahweh**. A very important **Ugaritic** text, commonly referred to as the "Baal Cycle," was discovered around 1930 and provides valuable information concerning Baal's identity and importance in the ancient Near East.

Babylonians—The nation of southern **Mesopotamia**, south of Assyria. Like the **Assyrians**, the Babylonians, too, spoke a dialect of **Akkadian**. Babylon's fortunes rose and fell throughout much of the second and first millennia BC until its rise to superpower status in 626 BC and its fall at the hands of Persians (King Cyrus; see Isa. 45:1) in 539. Their main role in Israelite history was their destruction of Jerusalem (587) and the deportation of the Judean population to Babylon.

Book of Biblical Antiquities—Likely written sometime in the first century AD, although some think a bit later. It is an ancient retelling of the Old Testament from creation to David and contains many examples of interpretive traditions. For many years it had been incorrectly catalogued among the works of **Philo**. Hence, the anonymous author is typically referred to as Pseudo-Philo. Along with *Jubilees*, it is a very important example of ancient retellings of the Old Testament, because of both its length and age.

Christotelic—A term that describes **apostolic hermeneutics**. The apostles understood the Old Testament to be moving toward the climactic event of the death and resurrection of Christ. They were able to understand this end (*telos*) only by knowing Christ and being illumined by his Spirit to see the true purpose of Scripture. This term is intended to be distinguished from the similar terms *christocentric* and *christological*. There is nothing wrong with these terms in and of themselves, but they have been used to express a very different notion, namely, that every verse, passage, or image of the Old Testament leads the reader to Christ or that Christ is in every last portion of the Old Testament. A christotelic approach recognizes that the Old Testament cannot lead to Christ without a preunderstanding of where the Old Testament is going. A christotelic reading is like a second reading of a novel. In reading a novel the first time through, the ending may catch you off

guard somewhat—not entirely, but certainly to a degree. But reading
the novel a second time will alert you to things that relate to that end.

Dead Sea Scrolls—Biblical manuscripts discovered accidentally by a
shepherd boy in a cave beginning in 1947. In the years to follow,
archeological investigation found a total of eleven caves that contained
more ancient scrolls dating from the third century BC to the early first
century AD. The texts found there are important on many levels.
(1) They contain the oldest known manuscripts of Old Testament books
(with the exception of Esther and Nehemiah, which are missing from
the scrolls). (2) The sectarian documents written by the members of
this community help flesh out aspects of their identity in the centuries
just before the coming of Christ and during his lifetime. (3) The scrolls
contain many examples of how this community interpreted the Bible,
and similarities can be noted with the New Testament authors. It is
safe to say that the discovery of these scrolls is the most important
manuscript find in modern history (pertaining to biblical studies, both
New Testament and Old Testament) and that they have had a profound
effect on our understanding of the nature of the transmission of the
Old Testament text and the world of the New Testament.

Deuteronomistic History—A theory that attempts to account for the
similarities in content and style among Joshua, Judges, Samuel, and
Kings. In 1943, the German scholar Martin Noth published the
argument that these biblical books form a single literary unit along
with the book of Deuteronomy and that these four historical books
reflect the theological concerns of Deuteronomy. He noted that the
centrality of worship in Deuteronomy is a recurring concern in the
subsequent historical books. Since Noth's time this theory has
undergone considerable reexamination, resulting in a number of
revisions and adjustments. His basic insight, however, has gained
widespread support.

Edomites—The nation located south and east of the Dead Sea. Genesis
connects Edom with Jacob's older brother, Esau, said to be the father
of the Edomites (Gen. 25:30; 36:1, 8–9, 43). In Numbers 20, Edom
refuses to allows the Israelites a passage through on their way to
Canaan after the exodus. The Edomites are also mentioned frequently
in the historical narratives of the kings of Israel. Very little is known of
the Edomite language, since so few texts have been found, but it is very
similar to **Hebrew** and **Moabite**.

1 Enoch—An important writing from the **Second Temple period** that
likely reached its final form in the first century AD, although portions
of it can probably be dated to the second century BC. The earlier
portions of this book were likely influential among Second Temple
authors as well as in the early church. It is an important window to

biblical interpretation in the Second Temple world while also helping
to clarify various matters of Jewish and early Christian theology.

Enuma Elish—A Babylonian creation story discovered in the second half of
the nineteenth century that has drawn much attention because of its
similarities to the first two chapters of Genesis. The text is called
Enuma Elish ("when on high") by modern scholars after the first two
words of the story. It tells of the god Marduk's conflicts with, and
eventual victory over, other gods and of his subsequent acts of
creation. The thrust of the story seems to be the justification of
Marduk's supremacy over the other Babylonian gods, and the text also
asserts the importance of Babylon vis-à-vis other Mesopotamian city-
states. The beginning of the rise of Babylonian supremacy and the
elevation of Marduk as the supreme god can be located in the early
second millennium, particularly with the reign of Hammurabi (1792–
1750 BC). The common view, therefore, is that *Enuma Elish*, at least
some version of the story, was well known certainly by the middle of
the second millennium BC.

Eschaton/eschatology—From the Greek word *eschatos* ("last, final"). In
popular circles eschatology often refers to various theories
surrounding the end of the world. This is not how the New Testament
uses the term, and it is not how it is intended here. The end (eschaton)
refers to the first coming of Christ. His coming inaugurated the last
days, in which the church has been living since Pentecost. More
specifically, the eschaton is a two-stage event. The first stage was the
first coming of Christ, and the second stage is his second coming. This
represents the tension in which the church exists: we are *already* living
in the last days, but the complete end has *not yet* come.

Exodus, date of the—One of two dates commonly proposed for Israel's
exodus from Egypt: 1446 BC and around 1280 BC. The former date is
derived from a literal reading of 1 Kings 6:1. (Solomon's temple was
built in 966 BC, "in the four hundred and eightieth year after the
Israelites had come out of Egypt.") The latter date is based on many
factors, most importantly the archeological evidence for the twelfth-
century BC destruction of certain key cities, which the Old Testament
attributes to Joshua in the generation following the exodus. Hence, if
the exodus occurred in the fifteenth century, there would be a
significant lapse in time before the conquest of Canaan took place.
There is no straightforward solution to this problem, and other
solutions have been proposed. The question of the precise date of the
exodus is seriously debated mainly in evangelical circles, since much
of modern scholarship either dismisses the historical likelihood for
any exodus of Israelite slaves from Egypt, or espouses theories of
Israelite infiltration of Canaan that bear little resemblance to the Old

Testament account of a relatively brief series of battles followed by conquest.

General revelation—As distinct from **special revelation**, the idea that God reveals himself in all his creation, not just through special means (e.g., prophets or miracles). Evangelicals typically consider general revelation to be subordinate to special revelation. Nevertheless, God is the creator, and all creation reveals his glory (Ps. 19:1). For our purposes, the question is the degree to which the general revelatory material we have looked at in this book should affect how we understand the nature of the special revelatory content of the Old Testament.

Gezer Calendar—So called because it was found in the town of Gezer and seems to be a text that refers to the cycles of the ancient agricultural year. It may be the oldest example of extrabiblical **Hebrew** writing, dating to the tenth century BC. Others think it is likely written in **Phoenician**, Hebrew's parent language, or refer to it by the more general designation "southern Canaanite."

Greek—The language that the conquests of Alexander the Great, culminating in 332 BC, caused to be dominant in the Semitic world, heretofore dominated by **Assyrians**, **Babylonians**, and Persians. As is always the case, cultures of the conquerors and the conquered intermingled. The most concrete manifestation of this Greek influence for the history of Judaism is the translation of the Old Testament into Greek (**Septuagint**).

Hebrew—The language of the Old Testament. From an archeological point of view, its origins can be traced no further back than the **Gezer Calendar**. Most scholars feel that Hebrew as an independent language did not exist until the latter part of the second millennium BC. The earliest evidence that exists to date for a Semitic alphabet (see **Phoenician** and **Akkadian**) is about 1700 BC, and clear developments in alphabetic writing can be traced from that point on. It is not until after 1000 BC that we begin to have considerable evidence for widespread Semitic alphabetic writing systems. At this point, it seems very unlikely that the Hebrew language we see in the Old Testament was in existence in Moses' day. At the very least, the Semitic alphabet itself went through dramatic changes from 1700 BC to the late seventh century BC. The Hebrew script in the printed versions of the Old Testament is based on the so-called Aramaic block script, which began to gain prominence after the return from exile.

Hermeneutics—A term that describes one's approach to interpretation. It is not the nuts and bolts of what you actually do with a text in front of you. That is exegesis. Rather, it represents one's broader understanding of what it even means to interpret. For the apostles, *how* they actually handled the Old Testament can be called exegesis and is very much affected by their Second Temple context. Hermeneutics concerns *why* they came up with the answers they came up with and as such operates on the level of philosophical precommitments. To put it another way, exegesis involves matters of exegetical methods; one's hermeneutic is an expression of one's interpretive goal. As I argued in chapter 4, **apostolic hermeneutics** was **christotelic**.

High places—Altars built for sacrifice on hills. Before the temple was built, Israel sacrificed on high places (1 Kings 3:2). After the temple was built, however, such practice was denounced as a form of false worship, that is, a Canaanite practice (1 Kings 11:7). The key difference seems to be that, before the temple was built, high places for the worship of **Yahweh** were acceptable. High places for worshiping Canaanite gods and any high place after the completion of the temple were condemned, as they seemed to encourage participation in pagan religious rites.

Innerbiblical interpretation—The phenomenon of a later Old Testament author interacting with an earlier Old Testament text or tradition. One example cited in chapter 2, the Passover law in 2 Chronicles 35:13, seems to be an example of an interaction with earlier texts. Such may also be the case with Ezekiel 18 and Exodus 20:5. Other times, it is not clear whether a biblical author actually has a text in front of him or is simply interacting with a well-known biblical tradition. An example of the latter may be Isaiah's use of the exodus tradition (e.g., 43:14–21).

Josephus—An important first-century witness (AD 37–100) to how the Old Testament was understood at the time. One of his major works, *Jewish Antiquities*, is an account of Israel's history written for the benefit of the Roman elite. This lengthy retelling of the Old Testament, like other Second Temple retellings, includes interpretive traditions that apparently reflected Josephus's own understanding of the biblical stories.

Jubilees—Written around the middle of the second century BC, an important early witness to the retelling genre of the Second Temple period. It covers Genesis and part of Exodus. The name *Jubilees* refers to this author's attention to divisions of calendar time. He is particularly concerned that the more stable solar year be observed instead of the fluctuating lunar year, thus making sure that the various festivals would be celebrated at the same times each year.

Mesopotamia—Similar in meaning to ancient Near East(ern). Technically it refers to the land "between the rivers" (Tigris and Euphrates), that is, ancient **Sumer**, **Assyria**, and **Babylon**.

Midrash—Medieval **rabbinic** commentaries on the Old Testament and the interpretive techniques that they employed. Midrashic interpretation is not focused on the surface meaning of the text, but seeks levels of meaning that take into account such things as peculiarities of grammar or narrative gaps. In this sense, all the examples of biblical interpretation we looked at from the Second Temple period, including the New Testament, are midrashic. Some argue, however, that the term should be reserved for the actual rabbinic commentaries in which some of the history of Jewish interpretive activity is collected. If this argument is followed, one can still designate Second Temple interpretation as "Midrash-like" or perhaps "premidrashic."

Mishnah—Codification of Jewish oral legal tradition around AD 200. The Mishnah is the basis for the **Talmud**, which includes later rabbinic commentary on the Mishnah. Although focused on legal matters, the Mishnah also includes many examples of **midrashic** interpretation as well as the transmission of preexisting interpretive traditions.

Moabites—The nation that descended from the first of two sons whom, according to Genesis 19:36–38, Lot's daughters bore him: Moab and Ben-Ammi. The Moabites were located east of the Dead Sea, south of the **Ammonites**. There are many references to Moab throughout the Old Testament. Its language is known to us almost exclusively from the Mesha Inscription. Of all the ancient **Semitic languages**, it bears the closest similarity to **Hebrew**.

Northern/southern kingdom—The time immediately after Israel's united monarchy (under Saul, David, and Solomon from 1050 BC to 930 BC). For many reasons, one of which appears to be preexisting tensions between the north and south, the kingdom divided along geographical lines after Solomon's death. The southern kingdom included the tribes of Judah and Benjamin, while the northern kingdom included the other ten tribes. In 722 BC, the northern kingdom came to an end with the invasion of Samaria (its capital) by Tiglath-pileser III of Assyria. The southern kingdom fell to the Babylonians under Nebuchadnezzar in 587 BC. The remnant of the southern kingdom returned under the edict of King Cyrus of Persia in 538 BC and rebuilt the temple in 516 BC.

Pesher—The Hebrew word, meaning "interpretation," that appears in the biblical commentaries among the **Dead Sea Scrolls**. In these commentaries, a biblical text is cited and followed by an interpretation of that passage. The interpretation is typically introduced by phrases such as "the interpretation of the matter" or "its interpretation." This led modern scholars to classify these texts as "pesher commentaries." The interpretive method reflected in these texts is discussed in chapter 4 above. The Qumran community interpreted biblical passages in such a way as to demonstrate the "fulfillment" of the OT text in their midst. Pesher is eschatologically oriented and, by modern standards, highly arbitrary. However, pesher also involves a very well thought-out interpretive scheme that employs, for example, a subtle and sophisticated use of hook words and even textual variants.

Philistines—Significant players in Old Testament narratives. Whence they originated is not clear, but archeological evidence suggests they came from across the Aegean Sea. They eventually settled in Canaan along the coast of the Mediterranean Sea and were a constant source of trouble for the Israelites. The word *Palestine* reflects the Greek name for the region after the conquest of Alexander the Great in 332 BC.

Philo—Alexandrian-born Jewish philosopher and biblical interpreter (approximately 20 BC to AD 50). His works reflect the confluence of the Jewish and Greek worlds in the centuries following Alexander the Great's conquest. He is perhaps best known for his allegorical interpretations of the Old Testament, whereby the plain sense of the biblical text (names of people, places, events) is taken to refer to higher or deeper realities.

Phoenician—Ancient Canaanite language that is the direct descendant of so-called Proto-Canaanite (or Proto-Sinaitic), which is the first Semitic language known to use an alphabet (around 1700 BC). The Phoenician alphabet is a later development from Proto-Canaanite, the earliest evidence we have dating to about 1000 BC. Phoenician is the direct ancestor to the alphabets of other **Semitic languages**, including **Hebrew**, as well as the **Greek** and Roman alphabets, from which the English alphabet is derived.

Pseudepigrapha—Modern collection of many and diverse ancient texts, many of Second Temple origin, containing writings of both Jewish and Christian origin. They are often attributed to some ideal figure of the past, whether an angel or an important Old Testament person. They often claim some level of inspiration. The term implies for some modern readers that there is an element of deception, that is, that the writers, by attributing their work to an ancient figure, were trying to fool their readers. This seems unlikely, however. It is more likely that this was an accepted genre of literature in the ancient world. For our purposes, the Pseudepigrapha contain many important texts that engage in Old Testament interpretation. Among the more important are *Jubilees* and the *Book of Biblical Antiquities*. Also mentioned in chapter 4 are the *Sibylline Oracles*, *Assumption of Moses*, and *1 Enoch*.

Qoheleth—The main character of the book of Ecclesiastes. It is unclear what this name means. It is translated "Teacher" in the New International Version, but that is dependent on the Septuagint's translation of Qoheleth as *ekklēsiastēs*. Qoheleth could come from the Hebrew word meaning "assembly," but that does not really help us in understanding what that means as the designation of a person. It is also unclear who the historical referent is. Qoheleth claims to have been king over Israel in Jerusalem, and so a common assumption is that Solomon is the historical figure indicated. This is considered by nearly all scholars as highly unlikely, partly because the style of the Hebrew in Ecclesiastes fits naturally into a postexilic context. It seems that Qoheleth is a literary persona employed by the anonymous author.

1QpHab—A scholarly abbreviation for the text and commentary on Habakkuk found among the Dead Sea Scrolls and signifying cave 1, Qumran, pesher on Habakkuk (see **Pesher**).

Qumran scrolls—See **Dead Sea Scrolls**.

Rabbinic—Developing Jewish tradition, surviving to this day, that has its roots during the **Second Temple period**. By no means a monolithic structure, the literature of rabbinic Judaism bespeaks a rich history of discussion and debate over many matters of religious practice and biblical interpretation. The main bodies of rabbinic Jewish literature are the **Mishnah**, Tosefta, **Talmud**, **midrashic** commentaries on biblical books, **Targums**, and many other works from the later medieval period. Since rabbinic literature is much later than the New Testament, its relevance to matters of New Testament interpretation of the Old Testament is a highly debatable topic. It is important to remember, however, that the date of *composition* of these texts has no necessary bearing on the antiquity of the *traditions* these texts contain.

Second Temple period—Technically, the period from the destruction of Solomon's temple in 587/586 BC to the destruction of the Second Temple in AD 70 (built in 516 BC). In modern academic discourse, this term is preferred over "intertestamental" or "postexilic." The former is considered to be prejudiced toward a Christian perspective, as it refers to the period of time between the two testaments; Judaism has no subsequent testament. The latter term is sometimes considered inadequate because it is too narrow. It really refers to the period of time more or less immediately following the return from exile and so cannot reasonably be used to speak of developments during the Greek or Roman period. Second Temple is the preferred designation because it is considered sufficiently neutral and covers a broad sweep of time. With respect to biblical interpretation, it covers everything from **innerbiblical interpretation** to the New Testament, which neither of the other terms covers.

Semitic languages—A family of ancient languages including **Akkadian**, **Hebrew**, **Aramaic**, **Ugaritic**, and several others for which there is limited evidence (e.g., **Moabite**, **Edomite**). "Semitic" refers to Shem, son of Noah, who settled in the area that would later become **Assyria** and **Babylon** (see Gen. 9:18; 10:1, 21–31).

Septuagint—Generally speaking, the **Greek** translation of the Old Testament necessitated by the conquests of Alexander the Great in 332 BC. An ancient legend, known as the Letter of Aristeas, tells the story of seventy-two scribes (six from each of the twelve tribes of Israel) completing the translation in seventy-two days, hence the name *Septuagint* (Latin *septuaginta*, seventy). This has very little basis in history. The precise origins of the Greek translation of the Old Testament are uncertain, although the Pentateuch was likely translated by 250 BC and the remainder of the Old Testament before the time of Christ. In contemporary scholarship, "Septuagint" is used to designate many things, which results in some confusion in the literature. For some it is restricted to the very earliest, original translations of the Hebrew; for others it refers to the earliest complete versions we have (fourth and fifth centuries AD); and for still others it refers only to modern scholarly editions. What is certain, however, is that Greek manuscripts of the Old Testament found among the **Dead Sea Scrolls** predate Christ. Greek was the international language of discourse by Jesus' day, and the existence of the Old Testament in Greek meant that Israel's story would no longer be restricted to **Semitic**-speaking peoples.

Sibylline Oracles—A collection of writings dating to between the second century BC and the seventh century AD and originating in various ancient cultures. "Sibyl" is the name of an old prophetess and is known to us from about the fifth century BC. She became a common figure in many ancient cultures, and into her mouth were placed prophecies of disaster for humanity. For our purposes, these oracles also contain pieces of biblical interpretation. Book 1 of the *Sibylline Oracles*, cited in chapter 4 in connection with the "Noah as preacher of righteousness" tradition, is, as all the other sections of these oracles, difficult to date with any precision. A broad range of years from 30 BC to AD 250 is suggested. That this author does not address the destruction of the temple in AD 70 may suggest a date prior to that, but this is inconclusive. Regardless of where we date book 1, however, the oracle's relatively lengthy section on Noah's preaching repentance is certainly not based on the incidental comment found in 2 Peter 2:5. **Josephus** also refers to this tradition in his *Jewish Antiquities*, which was composed in the last decade of the first century AD.

Special revelation—As distinct from **general revelation**, God's revelation in extraordinary ways, for example, miracles, prophecy, the Bible, and most importantly Christ himself.

Sumerian—The earliest known language of the ancient Near East, dating to 3100 BC. Sumer, located in southern **Mesopotamia**, was rich in its own cultural and religious traditions. Much of what we know about

Sumerian is learned from later **Akkadian** scribes. Sumerian is not a **Semitic language**, although its later written form is also attested in Akkadian: wedge-shaped characters (known as cuneiform) pressed into clay with a stylus.

Talmud—Authoritative compendium of Jewish legal tradition, specifically as a commentary on the **Mishnah**. The word *talmud* means "study" or "learning." There are two Talmuds: the Babylonian Talmud (fifth century AD), which eventually came to hold a greater status in European Judaism than the Palestinian or Jerusalem (third–fourth century AD) Talmud. The two are certainly connected, however, in that the Babylonian Talmud is dependent on the Palestinian. The dates of these works make their relevance to matters of New Testament interpretation of the Old Testament a highly debatable topic.

Targum—Aramaic translations of the Old Testament made necessary by the increasing popularity of **Aramaic** in the latter half of the first millennium BC. Portions of Ezra and Nehemiah are written in Aramaic. Like the **Talmud**, the Targums are placed into two groups based on their purported point of origin. The Palestinian family includes *Targum Pseudo-Jonathan*, which is a Targum on the Pentateuch. It is dated to the seventh–eighth century AD, but certainly contains many ancient interpretive traditions. It is an "expansionistic" Targum, meaning that its explanatory additions make it about twice the length of the Hebrew Old Testament. *Targum Onqelos* is also on the Pentateuch but is less expansionistic and holds a greater status. It is thought to have originated in Babylon, but this is not certain. It was probably finalized in the fifth century AD.

Ugaritic—Ancient language of a culture discovered in 1929 and located north of Canaan along the coast of the Mediterranean Sea in present-day Syria. The language is alphabetic and very similar to **Hebrew**, although it is written in cuneiform, like **Akkadian**. The literature found there is considerable and dates to between 1400 BC and 1200 BC. Among other things was found a story that features prominently the god Baal.

Yahweh—Conventional representation of the **Hebrew** "tetragrammaton" (four letters) for the name of God. The Hebrew letters correspond to English *yhwh*. Ancient Hebrew did not represent vowels in its writing system. A means of representing vowels was not introduced until the medieval period. Jewish tradition prohibited the pronunciation of God's name so as to prevent anyone from misusing that name (third commandment). Medieval scribes inserted vowels that made the divine name unpronounceable. Modern Western students of Hebrew, however, conventionally say "Yahweh." It is often translated "Lord" in English Bible translations, that is, in small caps to distinguish it from another Hebrew word for "lord."

Index of Scripture and Other Ancient Writings

Index of Subjects